The Spirituality of Fatima and Medjugorje

The Spirituality of Fatima and Medjugorje

by
Fr. Edward Carter, S.J.

Faith Publishing Co.
P.O. Box 237
Milford, OH 45150

The publisher recognizes and accepts that the final authority regarding apparitions rests with the Holy See of Rome, to whose judgment we willingly submit.

—The Publisher

Published by Faith Publishing Company

For additional copies of this book contact:

For bookstores: Faith Publishing Company
P.O. Box 237
Milford, Ohio 45150

For individuals: The Riehle Foundation
P.O. Box 7
Milford, Ohio 45150

Printed in The United States of America.

IMPRIMI POTEST: Bradley M. Schaeffer, S.J.

NIHIL OBSTAT: Edward B. Brueggeman, S.J.

IMPRIMATUR: Carl K. Moeddel
Auxiliary Bishop
Archdiocese of Cincinnati, Ohio
December 20, 1993

TO THE HEARTS OF
JESUS AND MARY

Table of Contents

Acknowledgments

The author acknowledges the use of excerpts from the following materials:

Scripture texts used in this work are taken from *The Jerusalem Bible,* Darton, Longman & Todd, Ltd., London, and Doubleday & Company, New York.

Live the Messages, by D.R. Golob, The Riehle Foundation.

Our Lady of Fatima's Peace Plan from Heaven, TAN Books and Publishers, Inc., Rockford, Illinois.

Preface

In these our times, there have been numerous reports of Marian apparitions around the world. Relatively few have received official Church approval. Among all the Marian apparition sites of the 20th century, two stand out as having received the most attention—Fatima and Medjugorje.

The Fatima apparitions and messages received official Church approval in 1930. In giving her official approval to the Fatima event, the Church tells us that what took place at Fatima involving the three young visionaries is worthy of our belief.

The Church's investigation of the events at Medjugorje is an ongoing one. No definitive judgment has yet been given. I hereby profess my willingness to submit to the Church's final decision in the matter.

In the meantime, one is allowed personally to believe in the apparitions and messages of Medjugorje provided they contain nothing which is contrary to faith and morals.

Millions do believe, including the overwhelming majority who have actually visited Medjugorje. Between 15 and 20 million pilgrims have been to this previously little known part of the world. Included in the Medjugorje pilgrims have been thousands of priests and numerous bishops.

Given the importance of the Fatima and Medjugorje events, we may legitimately ask, "Is there a very special connection between the two?'' Posing this question to myself and striving to find the answer has given rise to my writing of this book. I believe the connection is vitally important.

We live in extremely critical times. The Church and the world exist in a time which is witnessing an unprecedented alienation from God. During the 20th century Our Lady—as never before in history—has, through her numerous apparitions and messages, been pleading with the human race to return to God. Fatima and Medjugorje represent the high points of this urgent request on the part of Mary. It is extremely important that we listen to our Mother and do what she asks of us.

Edward Carter, S.J.
Xavier University
Cincinnati, Ohio

Part I
Fatima

one

Fatima: The Setting

On October 13, 1917, there were more than 70,000 people gathered in the Cova da Iria in Fatima, Portugal. They had come to observe a miracle which had been foretold by the Blessed Virgin to three young visionaries: Lucia dos Santos, and her two cousins, Jacinta and Francisco Marto.[1] Shortly after noon, Our Lady appeared to the three visionaries:

> As the Lady was about to leave, she pointed to the sun. Lucy excitedly repeated the gesture, and the people looked into the sky. The rain had ceased, the clouds parted, and the sun shone forth, but not in its usual brilliance. Instead, it appeared like a silver disc, pale as the moon, at which all could gaze without straining their eyes. Suddenly, impelled by some mysterious force, the disc began to whirl in the sky, casting off great shafts of multicolored light. Red, green, blue, yellow, violet—the enormous rays shot across the sky at all angles, lighting up the entire countryside for many miles around, but particularly the upturned faces of those 70,000 spellbound people.
>
> After a few moments the wonder stopped, but resumed again a second and a third time—three

times in all—within about 12 minutes. It seemed that the whole world was on fire, with the sun spinning at a greater speed each time.

Then a gasp of terror rose from the crowd, for the sun seemed to tear itself from the heavens and come crashing down upon the horrified multitude. . . . Just when it seemed that the ball of fire would fall upon and destroy them, the miracle ceased, and the sun resumed its normal place in the sky, shining forth as peacefully as ever.

When the people arose from the ground, cries of astonishment were heard on all sides. Their clothes, which had been soaking wet and muddy, now were clean and dry. Many of the sick and crippled had been cured of their afflictions.[2]

The above describes the great miracle which brought to conclusion the series of apparitions of Our Lady of Fatima which took place six times, from May to October 1917. The Miracle of the Sun was the sign God gave to the world in proof of the authenticity of the apparitions. The event was reported in newspapers around the world.

With one exception, Mary always appeared on the 13th of the month, above an holm oak tree in the valley named Cova da Iria. The only deviation from the 13th was the August apparition. During this particular month, Mary appeared to the children near the village of Valinhos on August 19. The children were in jail on the 13th of that particular month. The mayor, in an attempt to stop the events, had had the young visionaries kidnapped and imprisoned, but fearing violence on the part of the people, he soon released them.

Since the apparitions of 1917, millions of pilgrims have

come to Fatima. Fatima is a small, rural town about 90 miles north of Lisbon, Portugal. It is situated within hilly terrain which is lined with numerous cedar trees. The Cova da Iria—grazing ground at the time of the apparitions—now appears as a huge, paved area which lies in front of the Basilica of Our Lady of Fatima. About 50 yards in front of the Basilica, and to the left as one faces the Basilica, is the Chapel of Apparitions. Here, within the sanctuary, is a glass-enclosed statue of Our Lady of Fatima. The statue is situated on the spot of the holm oak tree over which Our Lady appeared to Lucia, Jacinta, and Francisco.

In the middle of the great square, one sees a large statue of the Sacred Heart. The arms of Christ are outstretched, welcoming all to come to the refuge of His Heart. Above the entrance of the Basilica is a statue of the Immaculate Heart of Mary. These two statues vividly remind us of the alliance of the Hearts of Jesus and Mary. As we shall soon see, this union of the Sacred Heart and the Immaculate Heart forms the very core of the Fatima message.

As is to be expected, the largest crowds of pilgrims gather on the 13th of the month from May through October.

I was privileged to be present at Fatima on a very special day, October 13, 1992. This date marked the 75th anniversary of the final apparition. It was, indeed, a most memorable occasion. On the evening of the 12th, there was the usual Rosary procession. Hundreds of thousands of pilgrims were present on this brisk October night. Pilgrims holding lighted candles, the praying of the Rosary, the procession with the Our Lady of Fatima statue—all this made for a very impressive and moving occasion.

The next day, the 13th, was obviously a very, very special time.

The day was bright and sunny with an almost completely blue sky. It seemed no accident. It was a gift of Our Lady, the Woman Clothed with the Sun: *Now a great sign appeared in Heaven: a woman, adorned with the sun, standing on the moon, and with the twelve stars on her head for a crown* (*Rev.* 12:1). We see, then, how fitting it was that the great miracle of Fatima described above was one involving the sun.

There were about a million people gathered in the huge square for this 75th anniversary occasion. The center of attraction was the Mass at the outdoor altar situated on the Basilica steps. Before and after the Mass, the statue of Our Lady of Fatima was marched in procession. The pilgrims waved their white handkerchiefs at the statue, a time-honored custom at Fatima. The entire ceremony took over three hours, yet there was a pervasive silence throughout the gathering of pilgrims, which numbered about one million. Their deep devotion was obvious. It was one of the most impressive and moving scenes I have ever witnessed.

During a stay at Fatima, one can always observe pilgrims visiting the Apparitions Chapel for Masses and adoration visits. Leading down to the Chapel is a special walkway which stretches back about 100 yards into the great square. This path is used by many pilgrims who, in an act of sacrifice, walk on their knees the length of the walkway, ending their journey at the Chapel itself. The atmosphere at the Chapel is one of deep peace and devotion, a common trait at Marian shrines.

Pilgrims are also constantly entering the Basilica for Masses and visits. At the front of the Basilica lie the remains of two of the Fatima visionaries. Jacinta's crypt is to the left, and Francisco's is to the right. Pilgrims stop briefly and pray at the crypts in a spirit of deep devotion. As one prays at these crypts, it is easy to recall the words of Jesus: *I bless you, Father, Lord of Heaven and of earth, for hiding these things from the learned and the clever and revealing them to mere children* (*Matt.* 11:25).

Central to the pilgrimage activities at Fatima are the many Masses which take place at the Chapel of Apparitions and the Basilica church. This, again, is a common occurrence at Marian shrines. Mary always leads to the Eucharistic Christ.

two

Fatima: The Message

Before receiving the six apparitions of Our Lady, May through October of 1917, the three Fatima visionaries were visited by an angel on three different occasions during the preceding year. He appeared to them in the spring, summer, and fall. Lucia (now Sr. Lucia) describes the springtime apparition of the angel:

> On reaching us, he said: *"Do not be afraid! I am the Angel of Peace. Pray with me."*
> Kneeling on the ground, he bowed down until his forehead touched the ground and made us repeat these words three times: *"My God, I believe, I adore, I hope and I love You! I ask pardon of You for those who do not believe, do not adore, do not hope and do not love You."*
> Then, rising he said: *"Pray thus. The Hearts of Jesus and Mary are attentive to the voice of your supplications."*
> His words engraved themselves so deeply on our minds that we could never forget them.[3]

During the summer of 1916, the angel again appeared to the three visionaries. He said to them:

> *Pray! Pray a great deal. The Hearts of Jesus*

8

and Mary have merciful designs on you. Offer prayers and sacrifices continually to the Most High. Make everything you do a sacrifice, and offer it as an act of reparation for the sins by which God is offended, and as a petition for the conversion of sinners. Bring peace to our country in this way....I am the Guardian Angel of Portugal. Accept and bear with submission all the sufferings the Lord will send you.[4]

In the fall of the same year, the angel visited the visionaries a final time:

The angel came...bearing a golden chalice in one hand and a Host above it in the other. The amazed children noticed that drops of blood were falling from the Host into the chalice. Presently, the angel left both suspended in mid-air and prostrated himself on the ground, saying this beautiful prayer: *"Most Holy Trinity, Father, Son and Holy Spirit, I adore You profoundly. I offer You the most precious Body, Blood, Soul, and Divinity of Jesus Christ, present in all tabernacles of the world, in reparation for the outrages, sacrileges, and indifference by which He is offended. By the infinite merits of the Sacred Heart of Jesus and* [the intercession of] *the Immaculate Heart of Mary, I beg of Thee the conversion of poor sinners."*[5]

Sr. Lucia relates how the angel gave them Communion:

Then, rising, he took the chalice and the Host in his hand. He gave the Sacred Host to me and shared the Blood from the chalice between Jacinta and Francisco, saying as he did so:

"Take and drink the Body and Blood of Jesus Christ, horribly outraged by ungrateful men! Make reparation for their crimes and console your God."[6]

Reflecting upon these messages of the angel, we see how much they contain for our spiritual instruction.

First of all, we notice the distinctive Trinitarian nature of the messages. We are instructed that, in our Christian existence, we must express the greatest reverence for Father, Son, and Holy Spirit, as we serve them through the virtues of faith, hope, and love. These three virtues are at the heart of our life of grace.

We are reminded of the ugly reality of sin and of our duty to make reparation for it. We are reminded that reparation is due Christ in His Eucharistic presence. And, as we shall soon see, Our Lady calls for a specific act of reparation—the five first Saturdays. Reparation is a foundation of the Fatima messages.

The angel also tells us that we must not only love God; we must also love our neighbor. We are to pray and make sacrifices for others.

In telling us to *"Pray a great deal,"* and *"Make everything you do a sacrifice,"* the angel reminds us that we are to live a deep spirituality. We are to be united with God throughout the day in as conscious a manner as possible. Regarding the angel's call to prayer, we shall soon hear of Mary's special request concerning the daily Rosary. It is a request that reminds us that God has sent Our Blessed Mother to call us back to Jesus, and to a closer union with Him. The Fatima message indeed reminds us that Mary is our spiritual Mother, that she is our mediatrix with Christ.

The angel specified a need to help others by our sacrifices, and to accept the sufferings God sends. It is a confirmation of Christ's paschal mystery of death-resurrection. The cross leads to life. We live the cross for the purpose of growing in grace ourselves, and in order to help channel grace to others.

The Angel also reminded us that the Eucharist is at the center of the Church's life. And, very importantly, in each of his three messages, the Angel drew attention to the critical role which the Hearts of Jesus and Mary play in our Christian lives:

> Another remarkable fact is that in each of the three apparitions, the Angel already mentions the Holy Hearts of Jesus and Mary, as though linked to one another by an indissoluble union. The account of the first apparition even presents a striking phrase which seems to have been hardly noticed. After having taught this completely God-centered prayer, *"My God, I believe, I adore, I hope and I love you,"* the Angel added: *"Pray thus. The Hearts of Jesus and Mary are attentive to the voice of your supplications."* We pray to God, and it is the Holy Hearts of Jesus and Mary that hear and answer our prayers! How could it better express the truth that we can only go to God and please Him by this unique and universal mediation?
>
> Similarly, in the summer of 1916, when the Angel announces to the three seers their future vocations, it is the Holy Hearts of Jesus and Mary that appear in the foreground as the inseparable mediators of the "Father of Mercies." *"The Holy Hearts of Jesus and Mary,"* he tells them, *"have designs of mercy on you."*
>
> Finally, the third time, in the prayer of

Eucharistic offering, it is by *"the infinite merits of the Sacred Heart of Jesus and* [the intercession of] *the Immaculate Heart of Mary,"* that the Angel begs *"the conversion of poor sinners"* of the Trinity.

With this constant thought of the mediation of the Holy Hearts of Jesus and Mary, we are already at the very center of the Message of Fatima.[7]

The Angel's three messages contain an amazing spiritual doctrine. The Angel gives the outline of the spiritual life within the framework of devotion to the Hearts of Jesus and Mary. **Behold, the spirituality of Fatima!**

The Angel's instruction to the three children admirably prepared them for Our Lady's apparitions. Mary's messages presume, and build upon, the spiritual doctrine which the Angel gave to the three young visionaries—and to us.

May 13, 1917, marks the first appearance of Our Lady of Fatima to Lucia, Jacinta, and Francisco. On this occasion, she said to the visionaries:

> *Do not be afraid, I will do you no harm. . . . I am from Heaven.*
>
> *I have come to ask you to come here for six months in succession, on the 13th day, at the same hour. Later on, I will tell you who I am and what I want.*
>
> *Are you willing to offer yourselves to God and bear all the sufferings He wills to send you, as an act of reparation for the sins by which He is offended, and in supplication for the conversion of sinners?*

> *Pray the Rosary every day in order to obtain*
> *peace for the world, and the end of the war.*[8]

To the end of each decade of the Rosary, she added the Fatima prayer, *"O my Jesus, forgive us our sins, save us from the fire of Hell, lead all souls to Heaven, especially those who have most need of Thy mercy."*[9]

In Mary's first message, we immediately see two aspects of the Fatima message—prayer (especially the Rosary) and reparation.

On June 13, the Blessed Virgin again appeared to the three children:

> There were about 70 people present, though only the children could see the apparition. She told the youngsters that many souls go to Hell because they have no one to pray and make sacrifices for them. She said Francisco and Jacinta would soon leave the world for Heaven. Holding out her heart, surrounded by thorns which pierced it from all sides, Our Lady told Lucy: *"God wishes you to remain in the world for some time because He wants to use you to establish in the world the devotion to my Immaculate Heart. I promise salvation to those who embrace it, and their souls will be loved by God as flowers placed by myself to adorn His throne."* [10]

This shows how devotion to the Immaculate Heart is central to the Fatima message. Subsequent events re-emphasize the importance of Our Lady teaching this devotion at Fatima.

In her July apparition, Our Lady further revealed her

plan to the children and to the world:

> During her appearance in July, Our Lady, in
> answer to Lucy's plea, promised that in October
> she would work a great miracle so that all might
> believe and know who she was. Again, the
> Mother of God told the children to sacrifice
> themselves for sinners and to say many times,
> especially when making a sacrifice, this prayer:
> *"O my Jesus, I offer this for love of Thee, for*
> *the conversion of poor sinners, and in repara-*
> *tion for all the sins committed against the*
> *Immaculate Heart of Mary."*[11]

During this same July apparition, Mary showed the
three children a vision of Hell. She told them:

> *You have seen Hell, where the souls of poor*
> *sinners go. To save them, God wishes to estab-*
> *lish, in the world, devotion to my Immaculate*
> *Heart. If people do what I tell you, many souls*
> *will be saved and there will be peace.*
> *The war (World War I, then raging) is going*
> *to end. But if people do not stop offending God,*
> *another and worse one will begin in the reign*
> *of Pius XI. When you shall see a night illumi-*
> *nated by an unknown light* [January 2, 1938],
> *know that this is the great sign that God gives*
> *you that He is going to punish the world for its*
> *many crimes by means of war, hunger, and*
> *persecution of the Church and the Holy*
> *Father.*[12]
> *To prevent this, I shall come to ask for the*
> *consecration of Russia to my Immaculate Heart*
> *and the Communion of Reparation on the five*

first Saturdays. If my requests are granted, Russia will be converted and there will be peace. If not, she will scatter her errors throughout the world, provoking wars and persecutions of the Church. The good will be martyred, the Holy Father will have much to suffer, and various nations will be destroyed. . . .

But in the end, my Immaculate Heart will triumph, the Holy Father will consecrate Russia to me, Russia will be converted, and a certain period of peace will be granted to the world.[12]

In the above, Mary speaks of the five first Saturdays. Here is what the practice involves:

1. Go to confession, which may be done from eight days before to eight days after the first Saturday. Of course, if a person is in the state of serious sin, the confession must be made before receiving communion.
2. Receive Holy Communion.
3. Recite five decades of the Rosary.
4. Meditate for 15 minutes on the mysteries of the Rosary.

   All of the above (except confession) must be done on the first Saturday of five consecutive months, with the intention of making reparation to the Immaculate Heart. For those who make the five first Saturdays, Our Lady of Fatima has promised to assist them at the hour of death, with all the graces necessary for salvation.[14]

Because of the excitement caused by the apparitions, the civil authorities were so alarmed that they kidnapped the three young visionaries and put them in jail. The incarceration period included the day of August 13. Consequently, Our Lady did not appear to the children on this particular 13th.

The authorities, fearing reaction on the part of the people, quickly released the children. Mary appeared to them on August 19 near Valinhos:

> She told them she was greatly displeased by the action of the mayor. As a result, the miracle promised for October would not be as impressive as originally planned.[15]

Next came the September appearance of Our Lady:

> More than 30,000 people were present in September, and saw a shower of mysterious white petals fall to within 10 feet of the ground before dissolving into the air. Many also saw the globe of light bearing the Lady come to rest atop the tree, and the branches bend as though someone were standing on them. Later, they saw the cloud depart into the east, from whence it had come.[16]

The October 13 vision was accompanied by the great Miracle of the Sun described in the previous chapter. In her message that day, Our Blessed Mother told the children:

> *I am the Lady of the Rosary. I have come to warn the faithful to amend their lives and to ask pardon for their sins. They must not offend Our Lord any more, for He is already too grievously offended by the sins of men. People must say the Rosary. Let them continue saying it every day.*[17]

While the people in attendance were beholding the great Miracle of the Sun, the three young visionaries, and they alone, were privileged to see striking visions in the heavens:

> As Our Lady had promised, St. Joseph had come with the Holy Family and had blessed the world. Then, Our Lady appeared as the Mother of Sorrows, accompanied by her Divine Son, Who also blessed the world. Finally, Lucy had seen the Blessed Virgin, dressed in the brown robes of Our Lady of Mount Carmel, crowned as Queen of Heaven and Earth, holding a brown Scapular in her hand, with her infant Son upon her knee. However, in none of these visions had any of the figures spoken to the children.[18]

Besides the messages associated with the major Fatima apparitions, there were other revelations given by Our Lady. Before Jacinta died, she told of other messages given her (during her illness) by Mary:

> *More souls go to Hell because of sins of the flesh than for any other reason.*
> *Certain fashions will be introduced that will offend Our Lord very much.*
> *Many marriages are not good; they do not please Our Lord and are not of God.*
> *Priests must be pure, very pure. They should not busy themselves with anything except what concerns the Church and souls. The disobedience of priests, to their superiors and to the Holy Father, is very displeasing to Our Lord.*
> *I can no longer restrain the hand of my Divine Son from striking the world with just punish-*

ments for its many crimes.

If the government of a country leaves the Church in peace and gives liberty to our Holy Religion, it will be blessed by God.

Tell everybody that God gives graces through the Immaculate Heart of Mary. Tell them to ask grace from her, and that the Heart of Jesus wishes to be venerated together with the Immaculate Heart of Mary. Ask them to plead for peace from the Immaculate Heart of Mary, for the Lord has confided the peace of the world to her.[19]

This last message offers us an excellent opportunity to summarize the Fatima message. It tells us "that the Heart of Jesus wishes to be venerated together with the Immaculate Heart of Mary."

At the center of the veneration for which Our Lord calls is the act of consecration to His Sacred Heart and to Mary's Immaculate Heart. As we shall see in Part II of this book, this consecration calls for a total gift of ourselves to Jesus and Mary. Such a gift, obviously, includes a willingness to incorporate into our lives the other Fatima teachings and requests. As such, consecration to the Hearts of Jesus and Mary summarizes the Fatima message.

Some seem to think the message of Fatima is no longer relevant to today's world. The words of Pope John Paul II tell us how wrong they are. Referring to a pilgrimage he made in 1982, he says:

Last week, I myself went on pilgrimage to Portugal, especially to Fatima, in order to give thanks that the mercy of God and the protection

of the Mother of Christ had saved my life last
year. The message of Fatima is a call to conversion and penance, the first and most basic call
of the Gospel. Today, it is more urgent than
ever, when evil is threatening us through errors
based on denial of God. The message of Fatima
puts us on our guard. It also invites us to
approach anew the Fountain of Mercy by an act
of consecration. Mary wishes us to draw near
it: each one of us, each nation, and the whole
world.[20]

CONSECRATION

Lord Jesus, I consecrate my life to Your most Sacred Heart. I believe You died for my redemption. I throw myself at Your feet, imploring Your Divine Mercy and Compassion. Through Your grace may I seek Your will in all things, in all aspects of my life. Most Sacred Heart of Jesus, I trust in You!

Dear Blessed Virgin Mary, you are the mother of my Savior. Accept me as your child as well. I consecrate myself to your Immaculate Heart. Teach me your humility and love for all mankind. Help me to always seek the peace promised us by your Son. Be my intercessor, that through your Immaculate Heart, I may be guided ever closer to the Sacred Heart of Jesus.

Jacinta, Francisco & Lucia in 1917.

Jacinta is carried after the miracle of the sun.
Crowds made it impossible for her to leave.

Photostatic copy of a page from Ilustração Portugueza,
October 29, 1917, showing the crowd looking at the dance of the
sun on October 13, 1917.

The Pilgrim Virgin statue of
Our Lady of Fatima.

Hundreds of thousands were in Fatima for the
75th anniversary of the miracle of the sun.

24

The Basilica at Fatima today.

Pope Paul VI came to Fatima
"as a pilgrim to pray for peace."

Sister Lucia 50
years after the
apparitions.

May 13, 1982. At the end of the Mass, the Pope consecrated the
world and Russia to the Immaculate Heart of Mary.
(Photo courtesy of Blue Army).

Vicka, Jakov, Ivanka, Maria and Ivan during an apparition.

The Church of St. James, Medjugorje, in 1983.

During the current war, Serbian aircraft initially attempted to bomb Medjugorje. The bomb did not explode, and was "planted" in a water drain outside of the St. James Church. At one point, it was adorned with a Geranium.

The visionaries, Vicka (top, center) and Ivan, continually meet with pilgrims at Medjugorje.

The huge, concrete cross atop Mt. Krizevac, at Medjugorje.

Mass at St. James is often con-celebrated by dozens of priests.

31

Painting of Lucia's apparition of June, 1929.

The Queen of Peace pilgrimage to Russia in October, 1992,
brought Our Lady back to the people of the former Soviet Union.

Part II

Fatima and Medjugorje:
The Point of Convergence

three

Conversion through Consecration to the Hearts of Jesus and Mary

Fatima and Medjugorje have been the two great apparition sites of Our Blessed Mother during the 20th century. They, in turn, were preceded by Mary's apparitions at Lourdes in 1858. There is an intimate connection among the three. Fr. René Laurentin, one of the world's foremost Mariologists, makes a very interesting observation: "Medjugorje is the Fatima of our day. The hours of the apparitions follow a progression. At Lourdes, they took place in the morning. At Fatima, at noon. At Medjugorje, in the evening. Is it the end of a long day...."[21]

Laurentin's observation suggests a very definite connection between Lourdes, Fatima, and Medjugorje. What is the point of convergence? At all three Marian sites Our Blessed Mother has called for conversion.

There are two basic types of conversion. The first type involves those who have seriously strayed from God. For these, the message of conversion is calling them back to the path of basic and essential Christian living. The second type of conversion regards those who are in an essentially correct relationship with God. Mary calls these to a deepening of their spiritual lives in Christ. Of course, those of the first type of conversion join those of the second kind after their return to the path of the Lord.

Christians have always been called to conversion throughout the history of the Church. Is there anything distinctive about Mary's call to conversion put forth at Lourdes, Fatima, and Medjugorje? Mary's call to conversion at these apparition sites centers in consecration to the Heart of Jesus and to her own Immaculate Heart. At Lourdes, the idea of consecration to the Hearts of Jesus and Mary is not explicit. However, it is there implicitly. At Lourdes, Mary identified herself as the Immaculate Conception, as having been conceived without original sin. The fact that Mary was preserved from original sin is coupled with the truth that she was also free of personal sin. The completely sinless one, in her motherly solicitude, calls sinners to reform their lives. Mary, the perfectly Immaculate One, points the way to a closer following of her Son, Jesus. She, who followed Christ perfectly, has given us a message at Lourdes, which, if lived, brings us closer to Christ. It helps us live out our baptismal consecration to Christ. Also, Our Lady of Lourdes has asked all of her children to entrust themselves to her and to her guidance—ideas connected with consecration.

If at Lourdes, Mary identifies herself as the Immaculate Conception, at Fatima, she appears as the Immaculate Heart. We easily see the connection. At Fatima, Mary draws attention to her sinlessness—the fact that she is the Immaculate One—in reference to her Heart. She appears as the most pure Virgin, who, in her sinlessness, possesses an Immaculate Heart. In this Heart, Mary loves God and us with an unfathomable love.

This certainly shows a major connecting point between Lourdes and Fatima, but there is a more profound connection between Fatima and Medjugorje. As indicated previously, at both Fatima and Medjugorje (and Lourdes), Mary has called us to conversion. Read again part of Our Lady's message of July 13, 1917:

> *You have seen Hell, where the souls of poor*
> *sinners go. To save them, God wishes to estab-*
> *lish in the world devotion to my Immaculate*
> *Heart. If what I say to you is done, many souls*
> *will be saved and there will be peace. The war*
> *will end. But if people do not cease offending*
> *God, a worse one will break out during the*
> *reign of Pius XI.*[22]

Because not enough people responded to Our Lady of
Fatima's request for conversion, the tragedy of World War
II did occur.

Through many of her messages at Medjugorje, Our
Lady is also calling us to conversion. It is emphatic, such
as part of her message of January 25, 1988:

> *Dear children, today, again I am calling you*
> *to complete conversion. . . . I am inviting you,*
> *dear children, to convert fully to God. . . .*[23]

As at Fatima, Mary's call for conversion at Medjugorje
is connected with world peace. Mary, Queen of Peace,
wishes to establish peace throughout the world, and she
asks us to help accomplish this great goal. We do our
part by living her messages—by living the life of ongoing
conversion.

Both Fatima and Medjugorje, then, have as their point
of convergence, the call to conversion. It is intimately
linked with the quest of establishing peace in the world.
This peace will take place when the human family is at
peace with God—when human hearts are united with
God, in loving conformity to His will.

Mary's call to conversion at Fatima and Medjugorje has
a very distinguishing characteristic. She calls us to con-

version by means of consecration to the Heart of Christ and to her own Immaculate Heart. The complete point of convergence between Fatima and Medjugorje is: **conversion through consecration to the Sacred Heart of Jesus and to the Immaculate Heart of Mary.** In other words, all the messages of Fatima and Medjugorje are connected with Mary's calling us to consecration to the Heart of Jesus and to her own Immaculate Heart.

The following Fatima message points out the pivotal nature of this consecration. Mary said to Jacinta:

> *Tell everyone that God gives graces through the Immaculate Heart of Mary. Tell them to ask graces from her, and that the Heart of Jesus wishes to be venerated together with the Immaculate Heart of Mary. Ask them to plead for peace from the Immaculate Heart of Mary, for the Lord has confided the peace of the world to her.*[24]

At the center of veneration of the Hearts of Jesus and Mary is the act of consecration to the Heart of Jesus and to the Immaculate Heart of Mary.

A statement by Archbishop R. Arulappa further reveals how the message of Fatima centers in the act of consecration to the Heart of Jesus and to the Immaculate Heart of Mary:

> In connection with the apparitions of Our Lady at Fatima, Sister Lucia, one of the seers, still alive, has been saying that on the 13th June 1929, Our Lady requested (as sister herself records in *Memoirs and Letters of Sister Lucia,* published in 1973), as follows: "The Good Lord promises to end the persecution in Russia, if the

Holy Father will himself make a solemn act of reparation and consecration of Russia... as well as ordering all the Bishops of the Catholic world to do the same.''

On March 21, 1982, Sister Lucia further explained to the Apostolic Nuncio, and two other witnesses, that the Pope must select a date on which to order the bishops of the whole world to make a solemn act of reparation and consecration of Russia to the most Sacred Hearts of Jesus and Mary, each in his own cathedral and at the same time as the act effected by the Pope.

There are actually two versions of the vision of Our Lady on 13th June 1929, but they are essentially the same. In the better known version, Our Lady says: *"The moment has come for God to ask the Holy Father to make, in union with all the Bishops of the world, the consecration of Russia to my Immaculate Heart. He promises to save Russia **by this** means."* The special mention of "Russia" in this Act of Consecration is to be noted.

When Sister Lucia asked Our Lord why He would not convert Russia without such an act of consecration, He replied:

*"Because I want my whole Church to recognize this consecration as a triumph of the Immaculate Heart of Mary, so as to **extend its** cult later on, and to place devotion to this Immaculate Heart beside the devotion to My Sacred Heart."*[25]

The above Fatima messages clearly demonstrate that the overall Fatima message centers, and is summed up,

in consecration to the Hearts of Jesus and Mary. The collegial act of consecration of Russia will occur, according
to Sr. Lucia "when a sufficient number are complying
with the message of Fatima."[26]

In other words, when a sufficient number are living the
Fatima message, as centered in consecration to the Sacred
Heart and Immaculate Heart, then the collegial consecra-
tion of Russia to the Sacred Heart and to the Immaculate
Heart will occur.

I realize that currently there is a dispute within the
Church concerning whether the collegial consecration
has or has not taken place. Some are of the opinion that
Pope John Paul II's act of consecration on March 25,
1984, fulfilled Our Lady's request. I myself side with
those who think that this particular consecration did not
totally fulfill all the requirements of Mary's request.

My main reason for taking this position is the content
of two of Mary's messages to locutionist, Father Stefano
Gobbi, spiritual director of the Marian Movement of
Priests. In these two messages, Mary definitely states that
the Collegial Act of Consecration, with all the conditions
requested by her, has not yet been made. The dates of
these messages are March 25, 1984, and May 13, 1990.[27]
The reader will notice that the March 25 date is the actual
day of the Act of Consecration referred to above—the act
which some say fulfilled Mary's request.

I myself believe in the authenticity of the Fr. Gobbi
locutions or messages. As far as I know, the Church has
made no definitive judgment regarding them, although
the Vatican does look with favor on the Marian Movement of Priests, and the messages of Mary to Fr. Gobbi
are at the very heart of the Movement. I hereby state my
willingness to submit to the ultimate decision of the
Church regarding the authenticity of the Gobbi messages.

The message of Fatima is centered in the request for consecration to the Heart of Jesus and to the Immaculate Heart of Mary. The same holds true for Mary's teaching at Medjugorje, as detailed in various messages:

> *Dear children, my invitation that you live the messages which I am giving you is a daily one. Especially, little children, because I want to draw you closer to the Heart of Jesus. Therefore, little children, I am inviting you today to the prayer of consecration to Jesus, my dear Son, so that each of your hearts may be His. And then, I am inviting you to consecration to my Immaculate Heart. I want you to consecrate yourselves as persons, as families, and as parishes so that all belongs to God through my hands. Therefore, dear little children, pray that you may comprehend the greatness of this message which I give you...* (October 25, 1988).

There are two points I wish to emphasize regarding this message. First, Mary connects all her messages at Medjugorje with consecration to the Heart of Christ and to her own Immaculate Heart. Second, she says, *"...pray that you may comprehend the greatness of this message which I am giving you."* In other words, Mary is saying that this particular message is a very crucial, a very pivotal one. She is saying that consecration to the Hearts of Jesus and Mary is at the very center of her Medjugorje teaching.

Later on, Mary gives another message regarding this consecration:

> *Dear Children! Today also, I invite you to prayer. Only by prayer and fasting can war be*

stopped. Therefore, my dear little children, pray, and by your life give witness that you are mine and that you belong to me, because Satan wishes, in these turbulent days, to seduce as many souls as possible. Therefore, I invite you to decide for God, and He will protect you and show what you should do and which path to take. I invite all those who have said "YES" to me to renew their consecration to my Son, Jesus, and to His Heart and to me, so that we can take you more intensely as instruments of peace in this unpeaceful world. Medjugorje is a sign to all of you and a call to pray and live the days of grace that God is giving you. Therefore, dear children, accept the call to prayer with seriousness. I am with you and your suffering is also mine. Thank you for having responded to my call (April, 1992).

And, in a very recent message, Mary tells us:

Dear Children! I want you to understand that I am your Mother, that I want to help you and call you to prayer. Only by prayer can you understand and accept my messages and practice them in your life. Read Sacred Scripture, live it, and pray to understand the signs of the time. This is a special time. Therefore, I am with you to draw you closer to my heart and the Heart of my Son. Dear little children, I want you to be children of the light and not of the darkness. Therefore, live what I am telling you. Thank you for having responded to my call (August 25, 1993).

We see the profound link, the profound point of convergence, between the spirituality of Fatima and that of Medjugorje. It is the ongoing conversion based on consecration to the Sacred Heart and to the Immaculate Heart.

Furthermore, we see the connection between Fatima and Medjugorje in the following fact. Although the Fatima message calls us to consecrate ourselves to the Heart of Christ and to the Immaculate Heart, it does not enter into great detail concerning all which this consecration involves. The message of Medjugorje does. Our Lady's messages at Medjugorje have been much more numerous and more detailed than those of Fatima. Now, she shows us all that is involved in living out our consecration.

Fatima initially outlined what is needed to save mankind. The messages of Medjugorje, while confirming the need, tell us in great detail how to accomplish it.

four

The Spirituality of Consecration

Before we discuss consecration to the Heart of Christ and to the Immaculate Heart of Mary, we should first establish what we mean by the word consecration.

To consecrate means to make holy. Only God can make one holy. Our fundamental consecration takes place in Baptism; in Baptism we are sealed with the holiness of God. The Persons of the Trinity communicate Themselves to us in a most intimate manner. They dwell within us and give us a share in Their own holiness. Through Baptism, we truly receive a participation in the divine life, and this sharing is our life of sanctifying grace, our Christ-life.

The reference to our life of sanctifying grace as the Christ-life reminds us that our being consecrated by God in Baptism is mediated by Christ. In fact, our act of being consecrated by God in Baptism is a participation in Christ's own consecration. A. Bossard develops the idea extremely well:

> By the Incarnation, in and of itself, the Humanity of Jesus is consecrated, so that in becoming Man, Jesus is *ipso facto* constituted Savior, Prophet, King, Priest and Victim of the One Sacrifice that was to save the world. He is the "Anointed" par excellence, the "Christ" totally belonging to God, His Humanity being

that of the Word and indwelled by the Holy
Spirit. When, by a free act of His human will,
He accepts what He is, doing what He was sent
to do, He can say that He consecrates "Himself." In Christ, therefore, what might be called
His "subjective" consecration is a perfect
response to the "objective" consecration
produced in His humanity through the
Incarnation.

And what Christ does brings with it a "consecration" for His disciples, a very special
belonging to God, since He imparts to them
His own life precisely by making them participate in His own consecration.

Through Baptism Christians also are consecrated and "anointed" by the power of the
Spirit. They share, in their measure, in the
essential consecration of Christ, in His charac-
ter of King, Priest, and Prophet (cf. *1 Peter* 2:9;
2 Peter 1:3-4; *Rev.* 5:9; etc.). With Christ and
through Christ, they are "ordered" to the glory
of God and the salvation of the world. They
do not belong to themselves. They belong to
Christ the Lord, who imparts His own life to
them. . . .

The vocation of those who have been bap-
tized is to "live" this consecration by a voluntary adherence—and one that is as perfect as
possible—to what it has made of them. Living
as "children of God," they fulfill subjectively
their objective consecration; like Jesus, they
consecrate themselves. This is the deeper
meaning of vows and baptismal promises,
together with the actual way of life correspond-
ing to them. The baptismal consecration is the

fundamental one, constitutive of the Christian.
All consecrations which come after it presup-
pose and are rooted in it...."[28]

The above details the awesome privilege and responsibility which come to us through Baptism. In Christ, we
are consecrated with the holiness of God. We do not
belong to ourselves. We belong to Father, Son, and Holy
Spirit, and through Christ, we are called to help continue
the work of the redemption. We have a mission to accomplish. We are called to participate in the prophetic,
kingly, and priestly mission of Jesus. We are called to
give an ongoing "yes" to our objective consecration—to
that which has happened to us in Baptism. This "yes"
is our subjective act of consecration.

To aid us in a special way in living our ongoing
"yes"—our life of subjective consecration—God has
given us devotion to the Sacred Heart of Jesus and to the
Immaculate Heart of Mary. At the center of these devo-
tions is a specific act of consecration. This act of consecration is a very special and attractive way to live out
our baptismal consecration.

Some may ask at this point, "Why the act of consecration to Mary? Is not the act of consecration to Christ sufficient?" Again, Bossard puts it very well:

> If, in the strict sense in question here, con-
> secration makes one belong to God—and Christ
> is God—how is it possible to speak of consecrat-
> ing oneself to Mary? It is possible because, by
> God's will, Mary has something to do with our
> Christian life, with our sanctification. She is
> certainly not, like Christ, the source of salva-
> tion, but she is maternally ordered to our life
> as children of God—always, however, in perfect

union with her Son and subordinate to
Him....Hence, in the full sense of the word,
a consecration to Mary includes, at least
implicitly, a real and essential reference to
Christ and to the Baptism that binds us to
Him.[29]

Jesus Himself has told us that He wishes us to
entrust—to consecrate—ourselves to Mary. We have that
striking and touching scene on Calvary:

> *Near the cross of Jesus stood His mother and
> His mother's sister, Mary, the wife of Clopas,
> and Mary of Magdala. Seeing His mother and
> the disciple He loved standing near her, Jesus
> said to His mother, "Woman, this is your son."
> Then to the disciple He said, "This is your
> mother"* (*John* 19:25-26).

Of course, the beloved disciple is John, who represents
all of us. In giving Mary to John as his spiritual Mother,
Jesus also gave Mary to us as our spiritual Mother. He
is entrusting us to Mary. He calls attention to the fact that
Mary is the Mother of our Christ-life, our life of grace.
In subordination to God, she gives us this life of grace,
nourishes it, brings it to full development. As she cooperates with the Holy Spirit, she assists us in living our baptismal consecration—the consecration which makes us
belong entirely to God in Christ.

Pope John Paul II has put before us the meaning of
Mary's spiritual motherhood on many occasions—in his
homilies, his acts of consecration, and in his writings.
In his encyclical letter, "The Mother of the Redeemer"
(Redemptoris Mater), he comments on the above Scrip-
ture passage:

It can also be said that these same words fully
show the reason for the Marian dimension of
the life of Christ's disciples. This is true not
only of John, who at that hour stood at the foot
of the Cross together with his Master's Mother,
but it is also true of every disciple of Christ, of
every Christian. The Redeemer entrusts his
mother to the disciple, and, at the same time,
he gives her to him as his mother. Mary's
motherhood, which becomes man's inheritance,
is a gift: a gift which Christ himself makes personally to every individual. The Redeemer
entrusts Mary to John because he entrusts John
to Mary. At the foot of the Cross there begins
that special entrusting of humanity to the
Mother of Christ, which in the history of the
Church has been practiced and expressed in
different ways.[30]

Yes, **Jesus** has given Mary to each of us as our spiritual
Mother. **He** wants us to grow in our appreciation of this
great gift by allowing Mary to be more and more Mother
to us. **He** wants us to grow in our entrustment to her,
in our consecration to her, so that she may lead us ever
closer to Himself. All this reminds us that Jesus has
willed that Mary be our Mediatrix with Him. Perhaps no
other devotee of Mary has emphasized this truth more
than St. Louis de Montfort. In speaking of this Marian
Saint, Fr. Authur Collings observes: "Perhaps, in the
final analysis, the greatest contribution of this Breton
saint to the theology of Marian consecration is precisely
in his insistence on Mary's mediation as willed by
God."[31]

St. Louis de Montfort, himself, emphatically reminds
us why we consecrate ourselves to Mary: "The more one

is consecrated to Mary, the more one is consecrated to Jesus."[32]

At both Fatima and Medjugorje Mary has asked us to consecrate ourselves to her in a particular way—consecration to her Immaculate Heart. Mary, our Mother, shows us her Heart as the symbol of her love. She tells us that she loves us with an overwhelming love and asks that we respond to this love by loving her in return, by making a total gift of ourselves—a total entrustment of ourselves—to her Immaculate Heart. She asks this of us so that she may be able to exercise her motherhood toward us as fully as possible. She wants us to imitate her own great love for Jesus, for the Father, and for the Holy Spirit. Her love for the Persons of the Trinity is symbolized by her Heart, as is her love for us.

A great sign of our consecration to Mary the Immaculate Heart, is the wearing of the Brown Scapular. Sr. Lucia, one of the Fatima visionaries, has said that we should wear the scapular as part of living the Fatima message. She tells us that "the Rosary and the scapular are inseparable." Our Lady, when she gave the scapular to St. Simon Stock in 1251, said, *"Whoever dies clothed in this shall never suffer eternal fire."* Only a properly authorized priest can validly enroll one in the Brown Scapular.[33]

How can we refuse the love and the loving request of our Mother? If we respond by consecrating ourselves to her Immaculate Heart, we can experience a remarkable sense of being loved, a sense of peace and joy, a sense of security and warmth. Resting secure within the Heart of our Mother, we are strengthened in all circumstances "to be for Christ"—to live out our baptismal consecration. Amid laughter and tears, success and failure, times of exhilaration and times of sorrowful disappointment, we can rest secure in the maternal heart of a Mother who loves us with an unfathomable love. If we can remain within the refuge of Mary's Immaculate Heart, nothing can prevent us from also growing in our consecration to the Heart of Christ. And this, indeed, is why Mary wants us to consecrate ourselves to her Immaculate Heart—so that she may lead us ever closer to the Heart of Jesus. This was emphatic at Fatima, and most certainly at Medjugorje.

In speaking of our consecration to the Immaculate Heart, Pope John Paul II stated:

> Our act of consecration refers ultimately to the Heart of her Son, for as the Mother of Christ, she is wholly united to His redemptive mission. As at the marriage feast of Cana, when she said, "Do whatever He tells you," Mary directs all things to her Son, who answers our prayers and forgives our sins. **Thus by dedicating ourselves to the Heart of Mary we discover a sure way to the Sacred Heart of Jesus, symbol of the merciful love of Our Savior.**[34] (emphasis added)

Yes, Mary the Immaculate Heart points to the Heart of Jesus and she wants us to immerse ourselves in the flames of this Heart. She wants us, in her company, to seek our refuge in Jesus' Heart. She asks us to dwell within her own Immaculate Heart more and more so that she may more and more place us deeply within the Heart of Christ. In all this, Mary cooperates with the Holy Spirit in forming Christ in us in ever greater measure. Her desire for us is that we grow in the likeness of Jesus, that we become, to an ever greater degree, Christians according to the Heart of Christ.

Devotion to the Heart of Christ is rooted in what took place upon Calvary:

> *It was Preparation Day, and to prevent the bodies remaining on the cross during the sabbath—since that sabbath was a day of special solemnity—the Jews asked Pilate to have the legs broken and the bodies taken away. Consequently, the soldiers came and broke the legs of the first man who had been crucified with Him, and then of the other. When they came to Jesus, they found He was already dead, and so, instead of breaking His legs, one of the soldiers pierced His side with a lance; and immediately there came out blood and water (John 19:31-34).*

It is interesting to note that St. John is the only one of the four evangelists to record this piercing of Jesus' Heart upon Calvary. How fitting! Jesus loved John with a most special love. John was the one who placed his head against Jesus' Heart at the Last Supper. John was the one to whom Jesus entrusted Mary and the one whom Christ entrusted to Mary as his spiritual Mother; John represented all of us. John, special recipient of Jesus' love, witnessed and recorded the piercing of Jesus' Heart, this heart which is symbol of Christ's love.

St. Bonaventure, a doctor of the Church, comments on how the Church was born from the pierced Heart of Jesus:

> Then, in order that the Church might be formed out of the side of Christ sleeping on the cross...the divine plan permitted that one of the soldiers should pierce open His sacred side with a lance. While blood mixed with water flowed, the price of our salvation was poured forth, which gushing forth from the sacred fountain of the Heart, gave power to the sacraments of the Church....[35]

From its roots on Calvary, devotion to the Heart of Christ has developed down through the ages. Numerous popes of recent times have highly recommended devotion to the Heart of Christ. One of the highlights of these papal affirmations has been Pope Pius XII's encyclical on devotion to the Sacred Heart, *Haurietis Aquas.* In speaking of the greatness of this devotion, Pius XII states:

> Indeed, if the evidence on which devotion to the wounded Heart of Jesus rests is rightly weighed, it is clear to all that we are dealing here, not with an ordinary form of piety, which anyone may, at his discretion, slight in favor of other devotions, or esteem lightly, but with a duty of religion most conducive to Christian perfection. For if devotion, according to the common theological definition which the Angelic Doctor gives, ''is apparently nothing else but the will to give oneself readily to things concerning the service of God,'' can there be a service to God more required and necessary— and at the same time nobler and more pleasant —than that which pays homage to His love?[36]

Pope Pius XII also speaks to us concerning Christ's Heart as symbol of love:

> Wherefore, the Heart of the Incarnate Word is rightly considered the chief index and symbol of the threefold love with which the Divine Redeemer continuously loves the Eternal Father and the whole human race. It is the symbol of that divine love which He shares with the Father and the Holy Ghost, but which in Him alone, in the Word, namely, that was made

Flesh, is it manifested to us through His mortal human body, since "in Him dwells the fullness of the Godhead, bodily." It is, moreover, the symbol of that most ardent love which, infused into His soul, sanctifies the human will of Christ and whose action is enlightened and directed by a twofold most perfect knowledge, namely the beatific and infused. Finally, in a more direct and natural manner, it is a symbol also of sensible love, since the body of Jesus Christ, formed through the operation of the Holy Ghost in the womb of the Virgin Mary, has a most perfect capacity for feeling and perception, much more than the bodies of all other men.[37]

Jesus shows us His Heart as symbol of His great love for us. This love is directed at each of us in a most precious, unique way, for He knows each of us by name. He knows each of us much, much better than we know ourselves. He loves each of us in our uniqueness with an incomprehensible love. In the greatness of this love for us, He hung upon a cross, His body racked with the indescribable pain of crucifixion; a body which had already been greatly weakened by the agony in the garden, by the cruel scourging, and by the carrying of the Cross. Besides the overwhelming physical pain, there was the agonizing suffering of His Heart. Part of this anguished suffering of His Heart was the knowledge that His love would be refused by so many down through the centuries. He knew that this love would be rejected so many times, even scorned and laughed at.

What is our response to Christ's love for us? With St. Ignatius Loyola, let us ask, "What have I done for Christ? What am I doing for Christ? What am I going to do for Christ?"

It is our privilege and duty to give ourselves to Christ. It is our privilege and duty, each day, to say "yes" to our baptismal consecration. Each day we have a renewed opportunity to realize that we do not belong to ourselves, but that we belong to God, in Christ. At Medjugorje, Our Lady reminds us of this:

> *Dear Children, today I wish to place you all under my mantle to protect you from every satanic attack. Today is the day of Peace, but throughout the whole world there is much lack of peace. Therefore, I call you to build up a new world of peace together with me, by means of prayer. Without you, I cannot do that, and, therefore, I call all of you with my motherly love, and God will do the rest. Therefore, open yourselves to God's plans and purposes for you to be able to cooperate with Him for Peace and Good. And do not forget that your life does not belong to you, but is a gift with which you must bring joy to others and lead them to Eternal Life. May the tenderness of my little Jesus always accompany you. Thank you for responding to my call* (December 25, 1992).

Each day is a precious opportunity "to be for Christ and others." Each day is a precious opportunity to renew that consecration to the Heart of Christ. In renewing that consecration, we can speak to Jesus in words such as these:

> Jesus, You have loved me so much. You continue to love me with a love whose depths I cannot fully comprehend. You have given and do give Yourself completely to me. Help me give

myself entirely to You. In myself, I am so weak and helpless. But in You, I am so strong. With Your grace, I make this gift of myself joyfully and gratefully. I make this gift of myself through the Immaculate Heart of Mary, the Heart of my Mother, this Mother who loves me so much, who has such a great desire for me to daily approach Your Heart. How much Mary desires that I immerse myself in the love of Your Heart! How eager she is to help me draw strength from Your Heart, in order to pour myself out anew in love for God and neighbor!

Jesus, I love You so much, and how much I want to grow in love for You! You are my salvation, You are my reconciliation, You are my happiness, my peace, my joy. You are my perfect Friend!

St. Margaret Mary Alacoque sheds further light on what is involved in consecration to the Heart of Jesus. St. Margaret Mary, to whom Christ revealed the secrets of His Sacred Heart, serves as a most eminent teacher for instructing us on how to live out our consecration. In a letter to a friend, the Saint says:

> . . . I shall simply tell you, as a true friend in the adorable Heart of Our Lord, Jesus Christ, that when I pray to Him for you, this thought occurs to me: If you want to live wholly for Him and attain that perfection He desires of you, you must make a complete sacrifice of yourself and of all that you have, without reserve, to His Sacred Heart. You must no longer will anything, but with the will of this most loving Heart, love nothing except with His love, act

only according to the lights He gives you, undertake nothing without first asking His counsel and help. All the glory must be His. You must thank Him for the ill as well as for the good success of your undertakings, always satisfied, never worrying about anything. As long as this divine Heart is satisfied, loved, and glorified, that must be enough for us.[38]

That we should give special attention to St. Margaret Mary's teaching concerning the Sacred Heart is confirmed by the following words of Pope Pius XII:

We mention, by way of example, the names of those who achieved special distinction in establishing and promoting devotion to the Most Sacred Heart of Jesus: St. Bonaventure, St. Albert the Great, St. Gertrude, St. Catherine of Siena, Blessed Henry Suso, St. Peter Canisius, St. Francis de Sales, and St. John Eudes. . . .

Among those who have promoted this most excellent devotion, St. Margaret Mary Alacoque occupies the chief place of honor.[39]

Yes, St. Margaret Mary holds a preeminent place in the history of devotion to the Heart of Jesus. I consider myself very privileged to have been able to make a recent pilgrimage to Paray-le-Monial. This is the French town where St. Margaret Mary lived out her religious life at the Convent of the Sisters of the Visitation. I was privileged to make a holy hour in the Chapel of Apparitions, the place where St. Margaret Mary received apparitions and revelations from the Sacred Heart. This was one of the most special experiences of my entire life.

St. Margaret Mary stated that Jesus has given twelve

promises to those who are devoted to His Sacred Heart:

1. I will give them all the graces necessary in their state of life.
2. I will establish peace in their homes.
3. I will comfort them in all their afflictions.
4. I will be their secure refuge during life, and above all, in death.
5. I will bestow abundant blessings upon all their undertakings.
6. Sinners shall find in My Heart the source and infinite ocean of mercy.
7. Lukewarm souls shall become fervent.
8. Fervent souls shall quickly mount to high perfection.
9. I will bless every place in which an image of My Heart is exposed and honored.
10. I will give to priests the gift of touching the most hardened hearts.
11. Those who shall promote this devotion shall have their names written in My Heart, never to be blotted out.
12. I promise you, in the excessive mercy of My Heart, that My all-powerful love will grant to all those who receive Holy Communion on the First Fridays in nine consecutive months the grace of final penitence; they shall not die in My disgrace, nor without receiving their Sacraments. My Divine Heart shall be their safe refuge in this last moment.[40]

In conclusion, we restate the fundamental idea of Part II of this book: **the point of convergence of the message of Fatima and that of Medjugorje is the call to conversion**

through consecration to the Heart of Christ and to the Immaculate Heart of Mary. The spirituality of Fatima and Medjugorje is a spirituality of **Hearts** and hearts—one which involves the Hearts of Jesus and Mary, and our own hearts.

Christ, the Sacred Heart, and Mary, the Immaculate Heart, manifest their great and unfathomable love for us. They reveal Their Hearts as symbols of this love, and They ask for our consecration in return. To say "yes" is to live out our baptismal consecration in a most special way. To say "yes" to Their request is our salvation. To say "yes" is to find the substantial and ongoing happiness we all seek. To say "yes" is to dwell secure in the Hearts of Jesus and Mary, where we feel loved and protected, where we find peace and joy, where we are fired with the determination to pour ourselves out in love for God and neighbor. To say "yes" is to go to the Father, with and through Christ, in the Holy Spirit, with Mary, our Mother, at our side.

Part III

Medjugorje

five

Medjugorje: The Setting

It was a very pleasant day—sunny with very moderate temperatures for late December. I stood alone on a section of Mt. Podbrdo, or Apparition Hill, as it is often called by Medjugorje pilgrims. Our pilgrimage group had just made the rocky climb to the site where Our Lady of Medjugorje first appeared to the six young visionaries— Mirjana Dragicevic Soldo, Ivanka Ivankovic Elez, Jakov Colo, Ivan Dragicevic, Marija Pavlovic Lunetti, and Vicka Ivankovic.[41] I gazed out across the Medjugorje valley which is surrounded by mountains. A very central spot in this panoramic view of Medjugorje is St. James Church. There, the church sets peacefully, with its two towers reaching heavenward.

Fr. Richard Foley, S.J., one of the internationally recognized experts on Medjugorje, says that whenever Mary appeared to the visionaries on Mt. Podbrdo, she would always be facing St. James Church, where the Eucharistic Christ resides.[42]

This fact tells us so much about Mary and her Medjugorje apparitions and messages. Mary always points to Jesus. Throughout the ages, she has done this. During her earthly pilgrimage, Mary gave us an extremely important lesson at Cana. Speaking to the servants at the wedding feast and directing their attention to Jesus, Mary says, *"Do whatever He tells you"* (*John* 2:5). Mary speaks these words to us today.

In her Medjugorje apparitions and messages, Our Blessed Mother calls our attention to the Gospel message. She is calling us to conversion with Christ, Who is the Way, the Truth, and the Life. Our conversion process never ends, for we can always turn more to Christ. We can always deepen our relationship with Jesus.

The astounding number of Medjugorje apparitions and messages tells any reflective person that we must be living in a very special time. In her April 4, 1985, message at Medjugorje, Mary stated: *"... The parish has responded, and I wish to continue giving you the messages, like never before since the beginning of time. Thank you for having responded to my call."*

Why is this such a special time in the world's history? Our Lady tells us it is because the world, in its sinfulness, has alienated itself from God as never before. God, in His great love and mercy, has entrusted Mary with an extraordinary mission. In her Medjugorje apparitions and messages—as she did at Fatima—Mary is giving forth her call to conversion in a most extraordinary and profound manner. She is continuing the messages and prophecies given at Fatima in 1917.

Mary, our Mother, loves all her children in such a profound way. In her maternal love and concern, she is again pleading with us to listen to her messages, to live her messages, so that we can help her lead the Church and the world along the path of conversion. We should ask the Holy Spirit daily for the grace to be open to what Christ came to give us. In this way, we will be instruments for helping to bring peace to the world—to be instruments which Jesus and Mary can use to help usher in a glorious new era of peace for the Church and the world—this is our glorious calling.

six

Love's Call to Conversion

A basic truth, which Mary very emphatically teaches at Medjugorje, is God's overwhelming love for us. She stresses that fact in many of her messages:

Dear children, today, also, I am inviting you to complete surrender to God. Dear children, you are not conscious of how God loves you with such a great love that He permits me to be with you so I can instruct you and help you to find the way of peace. This way, however, you cannot discover if you do not pray. . . . Thank you for having responded to my call (March 25, 1988).

Dear children! Today, also, I am calling you to live and to pay attention, with a special love, to all the messages I am giving you. God does not want you lukewarm and indecisive, but totally committed to Him. You know that I love you and that I am burning out of love for you. Therefore, dear children, commit yourselves to love so that you will comprehend and burn with God's love from day to day. Decide for love, dear children, so that love may prevail in all of you—not human love, but God's love. Thank you for having responded to my call (November 20, 1986).

How much does God love us? We can never fully comprehend God's fathomless love. We can, however, incessantly pray for the grace to better grasp and appreciate it. In our attempts to grow in knowledge of God's love for us, we certainly should include a consistent reflection on the well-known passage from St. John's Gospel:

> *Yes, God loved the world so much that He gave His only Son, so that everyone who believes in Him may not be lost but may have eternal life (John 3:16).*

Christ shows us His Heart as symbol of God's overwhelming love for us. A major aspect of devotion to the Heart of Christ is constantly to pray and meditate on the wonders of God's love, shown to us through Jesus, and always to give thanks for this boundless love. Devotion to the Heart of Christ—devotion to God's love for us—also requires that we be open to what God's love asks of us. It requires a response. In one of the above messages, Mary tells us, *"Therefore, dear children, commit yourselves to love so that you will comprehend and burn with God's love from day to day."* In telling us to daily experience God's love, she is instructing us to always appreciate most deeply God's love for us, His children, and to pray that we increasingly open ourselves to what this love asks of us. She is telling us to realize that being possessed by God's love is our happiness. She is reminding us that, to the degree a person refuses God's love, to that extent that person's life is unfulfilled.

In one of the above passages, besides speaking about God's love for us, Mary also tells us of her own maternal love for us. She stated, *"You know that I love you and that I am burning out of love for you."* She has repeated that theme many times at Medjugorje:

> *Dear children! I have told you already that I
> have chosen you in a special way, the way you
> are. I, the Mother, love you all. And in any
> moment, when it is difficult for you, do not be
> afraid. I love you even when you are far away
> from me and my Son. I ask you not to allow
> my heart to cry with tears of blood because of
> the souls who are being lost in sin. Therefore,
> dear children, pray, pray, pray! Thank you for
> your response to my call* (May 24, 1984).

> *Dear children! Today I will give you my love.
> You do not know, dear children, how great my
> love is, and you do not know how to accept it.
> In many ways, I wish to express it, but you,
> dear children, do not recognize it. You don't
> comprehend my words by your heart, and so
> you are not able to comprehend my love. Dear
> children, accept me in your life so that you will
> be able to accept all that I am saying to you and
> all I am calling you for. Thank you for your
> response to my call* (May 22, 1986).

Oh, how much our Blessed Mother loves us! *"...I
wish to give you my own love. You do not know, dear
children, how great my love is, and you do not know how
to accept it,"* she tells us. She is pleading with us to pray
for a growing realization of her immeasurable love for us
and for the light and strength to know how to accept this
love.

Mary, like her Son, shows us her Immaculate Heart as
a symbol of her love for God and for us. To grow in
understanding of that love, she asks us to practice devo-

tion to her Immaculate Heart, a devotion which is centered in consecration to her Heart. This consecration, as we have previously seen, involves a total gift of ourselves to Mary so that she might make of us a total gift to the Heart of her Son, Jesus. This complete gift of self to Jesus is our Act of Consecration to the Heart of Christ.

Mary's love for us also invites us to seek refuge within her Heart. Here, our ongoing transformation in Christ takes place, for the more we place ourselves in Mary's Heart, the more she places us in the Heart of Christ, where the Holy Spirit increasingly forms us in the image of Jesus. Within the Hearts of Jesus and Mary, we feel so much loved, so secure. We experience peace and joy. We feel strengthened for the ongoing task of helping Jesus and Mary further establish the Father's Kingdom.

The love of God for us, and Mary's love for us, are at the heart of the Medjugorje message. Mary tells us that through this love, They are calling us to do great things. We are being called to conversion—to that ultimate conversion which is complete surrender to God through complete consecration to the Hearts of Jesus and Mary. Mary tells us, *"Dear children, today again, I am calling you to complete conversion. . . .I am inviting you, dear children, to convert fully to God* (January 25, 1988).

seven

Holiness and Consecration

Dear children! Today, I invite you to holiness. You cannot live without holiness. Consequently, overcome all sin with love. Overcome every difficulty you meet with love... (July 10, 1986).

Dear children! I am happy about all of you who are on the way of holiness, and I am begging you to help, with your witness, all those who do not know how to live in the way of holiness. For that reason, dear children, your families should be the place where holiness is born... (July 24, 1986).

Dear children! You know that I wish to guide you on the way of holiness, but I do not want to force you. I do not want you to be holy by force. I wish every one of you to help yourselves and me, by your little sacrifices, so that I can guide you to be more holy day by day... (October 9, 1986).

In the above messages from Medjugorje, Mary very explicitly tells us that she has come to call us to holiness. Her call to ongoing conversion is a call to growth in holiness. Indeed, she calls us to complete holiness, to the highest holiness.

Here again, note the connection between the above Medjugorje messages and those given at Fatima. In 1917, Our Lady told Lucy: *"God wishes to establish in the world devotion to my Immaculate Heart. I promise salvation to those who embrace it."* On October 13, 1917, during the great Miracle of the Sun event, she stated: *"I have come to warn the faithful to amend their lives and to ask pardon for their sins. They must not offend Our Lord anymore, for He is already too grievously offended. Say the Rosary every day."* She calls us to conversion, reparation, consecration—in a word—holiness.

I wish to discuss holiness in terms of consecration, which we discussed in Part II of this book. Let's recall some of the ideas discussed there.

Only God can make us holy, and, at Baptism, He initiates us into the life of holiness. He objectively consecrates us—makes us holy—by giving us a participation in His own holiness. This participation in God's holiness is our life of sanctifying grace. In a response of love, we are called to say "yes" to this objective consecration. This "yes" is our act of subjective consecration. This "yes" is our allowing Christ to take us to the Father, in the Holy Spirit, with Mary, our Mother, at our side.

God consecrates us in Baptism through the mediation of Christ. Our baptismal consecration is actually a share in Christ's own consecration. Consequently, it is easy to comprehend that our life of consecration, our life of holiness, must develop according to the teaching and example of Christ. Our life of grace contains a Christic structure or pattern—it gives us the ability to think and act like Christ. Accordingly, our life of grace is often called the Christ-life.

In these our times, Jesus and Mary have called us to

live out our baptismal consecration through consecration to their Hearts. At Fatima, Mary called for this consecration. At Medjugorje, she has repeated this request. She has connected all her messages to the life of consecration to the Hearts of Jesus and Mary. Read again that very pivotal message which establishes this connection.

> *Dear children, my invitation that you live the messages which I am giving you is a daily one. Especially, little children, because I want to draw you closer to the Heart of Jesus. Therefore, little children, I am inviting you today to the prayer of consecration to Jesus, my dear Son, so that each of your hearts may be His. And then, I am inviting you to consecration to my Immaculate Heart. I want you to consecrate yourselves as persons, as families, and as parishes, so that all belongs to God through my hands. Therefore, dear little children, pray that you may comprehend the greatness of this message which I am giving you. Satan is strong and therefore, you, little children, by constant prayer, press tight against my motherly heart. Thank you for having responded to my call* (October 25, 1988).

I again want to emphasize two aspects of this message. First, Mary is connecting the living of all the Medjugorje messages with consecration to the Heart of Jesus and to her own Immaculate Heart. Secondly, Mary says, *". . . dear little children, pray that you may comprehend the greatness of this message which I am giving you."* Mary is telling us that this is a very critical message.

Our Lady of Medjugorje's call to a life of holiness is a call to consecration to the Heart of Jesus and to her own

Immaculate Heart. It is a carryover of her requests at Fatima. Growth in the life of holiness is growth in our life of consecration, and the messages of Mary at Medjugorje teach us what is involved in this life of holiness. They teach us how to grow in our life of consecration. They teach us how to say "yes" each day of our lives to what the Hearts of Jesus and Mary ask of us.

eight

Our Relationship with the Trinity

In Baptism, we are initially consecrated to the Father, Son, and Holy Spirit. So our life of consecration to the Heart of Christ is also a Trinitarian Consecration.

It should come as no surprise, then, that Our Lady's spiritual teaching at Medjugorje often mentions the Trinitarian nature of our Christian existence. Mary often speaks of our relationship to the Father, Son, and Holy Spirit. Many of the Medjugorje messages give evidence of it:

Dear children! Today I wish to tell you to open your hearts to God like flowers in spring yearning for the sun. I am your Mother, and I always want you to be closer to the Father, that He will always give abundant gifts to your heart. Thank you for your response to my call (January 31, 1985).

. . . Dear children, these are the days in which the Father is giving special graces to all who open their hearts. I am blessing you. My desire, dear children, is that you may recognize God's graces and place everything at His disposal so that He may be glorified by you. My heart follows all your steps attentively. Thank you for your response to my call (December 25, 1986).

71

My dear children, today I wish to invite all of you to decide for paradise. The way is difficult for those who have not decided for God. Dear children, decide and believe that God is offering Himself to you in His fullness. You are invited and you need to answer the call of the Father, Who is calling you through me... (October 25, 1987).

Mary, the Mother of Christ, knows that we cannot go to the Father without Jesus. Jesus, Himself, told us as much:

I am the Way, the Truth, and the Life. No one can come to the Father except through me. If you know me, you know my Father, too. From this moment, you know Him and have seen Him (John 14:6-7).

Mary loves to speak to us about Jesus. Her desire for us is that we grow in imitation of Jesus, that we come to reflect Him ever more in our daily existence. She wants us to live our consecration to the Heart of Christ at ever greater depths. At Medjugorje, she stated:

...Dear children, I desire you to be the reflections of Jesus, Who enlightens an unfaithful world which is walking in darkness. I wish that all of you may be a light to all and witness to the light. Dear children, you are not called to darkness; you are called to light and to live the light in your lives. Thank you for your response to my call (June 5, 1986).

Dear children! Open your hearts to the Holy

Spirit in a special way these days. The Holy Spirit is working in a special way through you. Open your hearts and give your lives to Jesus, so that He will work through your hearts and strengthen you. Thank you for your response to my call (May 23, 1985).

Dear children, rejoice with me. My heart is rejoicing because of Jesus, and today I want to give Him to you. Dear children, I want each one of you to open your heart to Jesus, and I will give Him to you with love. Dear children, I want Him to change you, to teach you, and to protect you. Today I am praying in a special way for each one of you, and I am presenting you to God so He will manifest Himself in you. I am calling you to sincere prayer with the heart so that every prayer of yours may be an encounter with God. In your work and in your everyday life, do put God in first place... (December 25, 1987).

Mary, as always, cooperates with the Holy Spirit in our ever greater assimilation to Jesus. This assimilation, this transformation, stems from Mary's Immaculate Heart. As Jesus was born of Mary by the power of the Holy Spirit, so we are continually being born of Mary in the Holy Spirit, into a greater likeness of Christ:

Dear children, I am with you even if you are not conscious of it. I want to protect you from everything that Satan offers you and through which he wants to destroy you. As I bore Jesus in my womb, so also, dear children, do I wish to bear you unto holiness. God wants

*to save you and sends you messages through
men, nature, and so many things which can
only help you to understand that you must
change the direction of your life. Therefore, little children, understand also the greatness of
the gift which God is giving you through me,
so that I may protect you with my mantle and
lead you to the joy of life. Thank you for having responded to my call* (March 25, 1990).

Mary knows very well that if we are to grow in the
likeness of Christ, we must abandon ourselves to the
Holy Spirit. The Medjugorje messages frequently speak
of our relationship to the Holy Spirit. Here are some
examples:

*. . . Pray to the Holy Spirit for enlightenment.
If you only knew the greatness of the graces
God was giving you, you would pray without
ceasing. Thank you for your response to my
call* (November 8, 1984).

*Dear children! You do not know how many
graces God is giving you. These days when the
Holy Spirit is working in a special way, you
do not want to advance. Your hearts are turned
toward earthly things and you are occupied by
them. Turn your hearts to prayer and ask that
the Holy Spirit be poured upon you. Thank
you for your response to my call* (May 9, 1985).

*Dear children! Today I wish to say to every-
one in the parish to pray in a special way for
the enlightenment of the Holy Spirit* (April 11,
1985).

Mary herself has a most perfect relationship with the Persons of the Trinity. She is daughter of the Father, Mother of the Son, and Spouse of the Holy Spirit. As our spiritual Mother, she longs for us to grow in our own relationship with the Divine Persons. We should always pray for the grace to fulfill her maternal wish. She has repeated it to us so many times—now, again, in these most urgent times.

nine

God's Will

. . . Therefore, little children, pray and seek the will of God in your everyday life. I desire that each one of you discover the way of holiness and grow in it until eternity. I will pray for you and intercede for you before God that you understand the greatness of this gift which God is giving me that I can be with you. Thank you for having responded to my call (April 25, 1990).

. . . I invite you all to decide for God, so that, from day to day, you will discover His will in prayer. I desire, dear children, to call all of you to a full conversion so that joy will be in your hearts. . . (June 25, 1990).

In the above messages, Mary talks to us about God's will. Indeed, this lesson concerning God's will is contained in all the messages, whether explicitly mentioned or not.

In Mary's school of holiness at Medjugorje, she teaches us about the Father's will and how to accomplish God's will in our lives. She tells us that it is God's will that we attend Mass, that we pray, that we do penance, and so forth. The messages teach us that it is God's will that we engage in ongoing conversion, that we daily grow in holiness. The Medjugorje messages teach us that it is the

Divine Will that we grow in our life of consecration to God which began at Baptism. Through our consecration to the Heart of Christ and to the Immaculate Heart, we are called to say "yes" to God's consecration of us. It is our ongoing "yes" to God's will.

Mary's own life is summed up in her loving conformity to God's will. The "Fiat" she uttered at the Annunciation sums up her attitude before this momentous occasion, during it, and forever after it: *" 'I am the handmaid of the Lord,' said Mary, 'let what you have said be done to me.' And the angel left her"* (*Luke* 1:38).

Mary was the first and perfect disciple of Jesus. She always perfectly accomplished the Father's will. She was Jesus' closest follower. She perfectly lived His message—which is summed up in loving conformity to God's will. Jesus Himself taught us this lesson by both word and example. Toward the end of the great Sermon on the Mount in Matthew's Gospel, Christ sums up the teaching of the Sermon in this way: *"It is not those who say to me, 'Lord, Lord,' who will enter the kingdom of Heaven, but the person who does the will of my Father in Heaven"* (*Matt.* 7:21).

Christ perfectly lived this lesson Himself:

> *When you have lifted up the Son of Man, then you will know that I am he and that I do nothing of myself: what the Father has taught me is what I preach; He who sent me is with me and has not left me to myself, for I always do what pleases Him* (*John* 8:28-29).

Yes, Jesus always did what pleased His Father. In love, He always did the Father's will. At that most special moment of His life, as He was about to offer His life in sacrifice upon the Cross for the salvation of the world, He again showed us that His conformity in love to His Father's will was the summary principle of His existence. As He knelt in the Garden of Gethsemane, as His terrible agony caused Him to sweat blood. *"Father,"* He said, *"if You are willing, take this cup away from me. Nevertheless, let Your will be done, not mine"* (*Luke* 22:42-43).

All the great spiritual guides, down through the ages, true to their Master's teaching, have taught that growth in the spiritual life—growth in holiness—is always measured by growth in loving conformity to God's will. One of these, St. Teresa of Avila, says:

> All that the beginner in prayer has to do—and you must not forget this, for it is very important—is to labour and to be resolute and prepare himself with all possible diligence to bring his will in conformity with the will of God. As I shall say later, you may be quite sure that this comprises the very greatest perfection which can be attained on the spiritual road![43]

And, again she says: "...love consists...in the firmness of our determination to try to please God in everything."[44]

In one of the Medjugorje messages quoted above, Our Lady says, *"I invite you all to decide for God, so that, from day to day, you will discover His will in prayer."* Each day we should pray for that light and strength to act according to God's will. Acting according to God's will—despite the very significant suffering this, at times, brings us—is our satisfaction and our salvation, our joy, our happiness and our peace. Mary continues to echo this Gospel call.

ten

Christian Virtues

The spiritual life—our life of consecration—is rooted in the exercise of faith, hope, and love. All the other virtues are variously in support of these three. We will say a few words about four of the Christian virtues—faith, hope, love, and also humility.

Faith

Faith is certainly included in many of the Medjugorje messages. Two examples follow:

> *Dear children! Open your hearts to the Holy Spirit in a special way these days. The Holy Spirit is working in a special way through you. Open your hearts and give your lives to Jesus so that He will work through your hearts and strengthen you in faith* (May 23, 1985).

> *Dear children, God wants to make you holy. Therefore, through me, He is inviting you to complete surrender. Let Holy Mass be your life. Understand that Church is God's palace, the place in which I gather you and want to show you the way to God. Come and pray. Neither look at others nor slander them, but, rather, let your life be a testimony on the way of holiness. Churches deserve respect and are set apart as*

*holy because God, Who became man, dwells in
them day and night. Therefore, little children,
believe and pray that the Father increase your
faith, and then ask for whatever you need* (April
25, 1988).

Faith, as St. Thomas Aquinas states, connects us to the
divine knowing. Through faith, we share in God's vision
of reality. Obviously, there is an infinite gap between
God's knowledge of Himself and His creation and our own
knowledge regarding the same. Nevertheless, supernatural
faith gives us a very special sharing in the divine knowing.

The contemporary Christian does not live in an age
conspicuous for its strong religious faith. Long ago, in
the golden age of Christendom, there was much more of
a Christian faith-milieu. Many with whom one lived and
worked were fellow believers. Today, a considerable part
of our culture is not only non-Christian, but also
secularistic and hostile to any religious belief. Addition-
ally, the present-day Christian has to face the distinct pos-
sibility of non-belief within his or her own family circle.
The theologian Karl Rahner observes:

> A Christian's faith is not a purely private con-
> cern. We live in the community of faith which
> is called the Church, but in practice we are a
> "diaspora" everywhere today, sometimes even
> among our own relatives...I mean that quite a
> number of people in our environment—let us
> face it—have, in effect, lost the faith, some of
> them becoming real enemies to the Church and
> officially leaving her.[45]

Whatever the problems and difficulties relative to faith
may be, we know that God sustains the person of faith,

in this or any age, if that person cooperates with His graces. God distributes His grace proportionate to the difficulties which confront the believer. On our part, we must pray. Let's not forget what Mary tells us in one of the above messages: *"Therefore, little children, believe and pray that the Father increases your faith...."*

Hope

Hope gives us both the desire to live according to the vision of faith and the trust that God will aid us in living that life of faith. Trust is a very important aspect of the virtue of hope. The more we progress in the spiritual life, the more we must trust in God. God has given us Mary as our Mother, to help us grow in trust. When we trust in Mary, we are ultimately trusting in God. At Medjugorje, Mary speaks to us about this trust in her:

> *Dear children, I invite you to prayer now when Satan is strong and wishes to make as many souls as possible his own. Pray, dear children, and have more trust in me, because I am here in order to help you and to guide you on a new path toward a new life. Therefore, dear little children, listen and live what I tell you, because it is important for you, when I shall not be with you any longer, that you remember my words and all that I told you. I call you to begin to change your life from the beginning and that you decide for conversion, not with words, but with your life. Thank you for having responded to my call* (October 25, 1992).

Love

Love is the queen of the virtues. All the other Christian virtues are geared to the growth of love within us. The primacy of love is magnificently brought out by St. Paul:

> *If I have all the eloquence of men or of angels, but speak without love, I am simply a gong booming or a cymbal clashing. If I have the gift of prophecy, understanding all the mysteries there are, and knowing everything, and if I have faith in all its fullness, to move mountains, but without love, then I am nothing at all. If I give away all that I possess, piece by piece, and if I even let them take my body to burn it, but am without love, it will do me no good whatever. . . .*
>
> *In short, there are three things that last: faith, hope and love; and the greatest of these is love* (*1 Cor.* 13).

As the virtue of faith gives us a sharing in God's knowing activity, so the virtue of love gives us a sharing in God's loving activity.

Many of Mary's messages at Medjugorje speak of love. In this message, our Mother, in a sense, startles us by saying we know little about love:

> *Dear children! You do not know how to love, and you do not know how to listen with love to the words I am giving you. Be aware, my beloved, that I am your Mother and that I have come to the Earth to teach you how to listen out of love, how to pray out of love, and not out of compulsion of the cross you are carrying. Through the cross, God is being glorified in every man* (November 29, 1984).

If Mary chides us for our lack of knowledge concerning

love, she also reminds us that with love we are great:

> *Dear Children! Today I call you to live the words this week: "I love God!" Dear children, with love, you will achieve everything, and even what you think is impossible. God wants this parish to belong to Him completely. And I want that, too* (February 28, 1985).

Love is at the very center of our consecration to the Heart of Jesus and to the Immaculate Heart of Mary. It is central to the Gospels. We grow in our consecration and say "yes" to Jesus and Mary to the extent that we love God and neighbor. Jesus and Mary invite us, each day, to enter the refuge of Their Hearts. There, they increasingly teach us the lesson of love. There, they more deeply engrave upon our hearts the truth that to live according to God's plan is to love. Remember Mary's words to us: *". . . but without love you will attain nothing,"* and *"with love you will achieve everything, and even what you think is impossible."*

Humility

Humility is added here because it is one of the chief supports of faith, hope, and love. Humility enables us to act on the truth that we are creatures of God and that without Him we are helpless. Humility prompts us to give credit to God for all the gifts we have received. St. Paul sharply reminds us: *"What do you have that was not given to you? And if it was given, how can you boast as though it were not?"* (*1 Cor.* 4:7).

Our Lady of Medjugorje also speaks to us about humility:

> *Dear children! Today I give you the message through which I am calling you to humility.*

These days you have felt great joy because of all the people who are coming, and you have spoken about your experiences with love. Now I call you to continue in humility and with an open heart to speak to all those who are coming (June 27, 1985).

Dear children! Today, I am calling you to live in humility all the messages I give you. Dear children, do not glorify yourselves when living the messages by saying: "I live the messages." If you carry the messages in your heart and live them, everyone will realize this, so there is no need for words which serve only those who do not hear. For you, it is not necessary to speak. For you, my dear children, it is necessary to live and witness by your lives (September 19, 1985).

Each day, let's ask Our Blessed Mother for an increase, not only in faith, hope, love, and humility, but also for growth in the other Christian virtues. And as we grow in the life of the Christian virtues, Our Mother smiles and looks with pride upon us, knowing that, as we progress along the road of holiness, we are increasingly becoming fit instruments in Jesus' hands and her hands. We are increasingly fulfilling our great role in helping to bring about the glorious renewal of the Church and the world.

eleven

The Church

Dear children! Today I wish to call you to work in the Church. I do love you equally. I want you to work as much as you can in the Church. I know, dear children, that you can work but you do not want to work because you feel that you are unworthy of the duties. You have to be courageous. As with little flowers, you enrich the Church and Jesus so that we can all be happy (October 31, 1985).

. . . I wish that each of you decides himself for a change of life and that each of you works more in the Church, not through words and thoughts but through example, so that your life may be a joyful testimony for Jesus. You cannot say that you are converted, because your life must become a daily conversion.

In order to understand what you have to do, little children, pray and God will give you what you concretely have to do and where you have to change. . . (February 25, 1993).

We live out our life of consecration to the Heart of Christ and to the Immaculate Heart within the Church. Let's remember a very important point we established earlier. Our original and fundamental consecration occurs in Baptism. All other consecrations are means for living out our baptismal consecration. The call of Jesus and Mary to consecrate ourselves to Their Hearts is an extraordinary gift given to us so that we may live out—ideally to the heights of sanctity—our baptismal consecration.

Our baptismal consecration has incorporated us into the Church. We are members of the Mystical Body of Christ. Christ, the Head, has established His Church as His Mystical Body in order to carry out His mission on earth until the end of time. The Church, drawing Her life from Christ, Her Head, prolongs upon earth the priestly, prophetic and kingly offices of Jesus.

In the above quoted messages, Mary reminds us that we each have a role in the Church's life. She wants us to do our share in the life of the Church because she deeply loves the Church and deeply loves each of us who are members of the Mystical Body. Mary is Mother of the Church and Mother of each of us within the Church. She is also Model of the Church. Pope John Paul II combines all these truths about Mary:

> Mary is present in the Church as the Mother of Christ, and at the same time as that Mother whom Christ, in the mystery of the Redemption, gave to humanity in the person of the Apostle John. Thus, in her new motherhood, in the Spirit, Mary embraces each and every one *in* the Church, and embraces each and every one *through* the Church. In this sense, Mary, Mother of the Church, is also the Church's model. Indeed, as Paul VI hopes and asks, the Church must draw from the Virgin Mother of God the most authentic form of perfect imitation of Christ.[46]

Our Lady of Medjugorje realizes how important it is that each of us fulfill his or her role in the life of the Church. What we do *does* make a difference. Vatican II, in speaking of the Church, reminds us: "Consequently, if one member suffers anything, all the members suffer it, too; and if one member is honored, all the members rejoice together."[47]

Whatever we do, for better or for worse, in some way, affects the whole Church. And not only do our actions affect the other members of the Church; they also reach out and affect those outside the Church. To the extent that members of the Church are living the way God wants them to live, the Church is better able to be a light to all nations. In so far as the Church's children are not what they should be, the Church is less able to fulfill her mission in the world.

Today, the Church and the world are passing through their most critical time. Mary is telling us that an unprecedented wave of sin is sweeping through the world, causing a situation never before experienced by the human race. Hence, the unprecedented number of Marian apparitions and messages are reported. Her prophecy given at Fatima was most explicit:

> *If my requests are listened to, Russia will be converted and there will be peace. If not, she will spread her errors around the world, provoking wars and persecutions against the Church; many good souls will be martyred, the Holy Father will have much to suffer; many nations will be destroyed.*

In this extraordinarily critical stage of the world's history, God is using extraordinary means to call the Church and the world to conversion. He is permitting Mary to appear at various sites around the world so that she, in her maternal concern, can give us God's call to conversion.

The Church, and through her the world, will be renewed. Mary is giving us this message. She is telling us that, through the pervasive darkness which sin has spread all over the world, the light of her Immaculate Heart is shining ever more brightly. This light is leading the Church and the world to an unprecedented relationship to Christ, the Light of the world. When the Church's and the world's purification have been achieved, the Immaculate Heart of Mary will gloriously triumph (as promised at Fatima) and usher in a new age of peace in which Christ, the Sacred Heart, will reign supreme.

Yes, Mary is telling us what is and what will be. She is telling us that the renewal of the Church is necessary for the renewal of the world. Our Mother says that each of us has a role to play in the life of the Church—a role which no one else can fulfill. She says that she needs your assistance and my assistance to help her bring about God's glorious plan. What is our response?

twelve

The Mass and the Sacrament of Reconciliation

*Dear Children! I am calling you to more atten-
tive prayer and more participation in the Mass.
I wish you to experience God within yourselves
at Mass. . .* (May 16, 1985).

*Dear children! I wish to call you to live the
Holy Mass. There are many of you who have
experienced the beauty of the Mass, but there
are some who come unwillingly. I have chosen
you, dear children, and Jesus is giving you His
graces in the Holy Mass. Therefore, consciously
live the Holy Mass. Let every coming to Holy
Mass be joyful. Come with love and accept the
Holy Mass* (April 3, 1986).

My pilgrimage to Medjugorje included the privilege of
meeting with Vicka, one of the visionaries. She told our
group that Mary reminds us that the Mass is the holiest
time of our lives. The Mass is the chief source of grace
for our growth in consecration to the Heart of Jesus and
to the Immaculate Heart of Mary.

Mary tells us to live the Mass. Before we discuss what
this means, let's discuss some ideas about the Mass.

The sacrifice of the Mass, as we well know, makes truly

present the sacrifice of Calvary. At His sacrifice on Calvary, Christ was Priest and Victim. We obviously did not
offer together with Him. At the Mass, however, Christ,
although He is the chief Priest and Victim, does not act
alone. Through God's gracious design, at Mass all the
members of the Church are priests and victims together
with Christ. To be sure, there is a very significant difference between the priesthood of bishops and priests and
the universal priesthood of the faithful. This difference
is one of essence and not merely degree. The point we
wish to stress, however, is that the universal priesthood,
given in Baptism to all the faithful, is a real participation
in Christ's priesthood.

Vatican II has stressed this concept of the priesthood
of all the Church's members. Speaking of the Mass, the
Council says:

> The Church, therefore, earnestly desires that
> Christ's faithful, when present at this mystery of
> faith, should not be there as strangers or silent
> spectators. On the contrary, through a proper
> appreciation of the rites and prayers, they should
> participate knowingly, devoutly, and actively.
> They should be instructed by God's word and be
> refreshed at the table of the Lord's body; they
> should give thanks to God; by offering the
> Immaculate Victim, not only through the hands
> of the priest, but also with him, they should learn
> to offer themselves too. Through Christ the Medi-
> ator, they should be drawn, day by day, into ever
> closer union with God and with each other, so
> that finally God may be all in all.[48]

When Our Lady of Medjugorje tells us *"to live the Holy
Mass,"* and *"Let Holy Mass be your life,"* we can see

the great truths she is encouraging us to live. Not only during the Mass itself are we all priests and victims, together with Christ, but also throughout our daily lives.

During all our Christ-like activities, we are living the Mass. Working, recreating, laughing, crying, enjoying success but also experiencing failure, enjoying the beauties of nature—through all such activities—we are living the Mass. We are continuously offering ourselves in loving conformity to the Father's will. From time to time during the day, we should make a conscious act of uniting ourselves and our activities with the sacrifice of Calvary as it is made present in Masses throughout the world.

A very precious time during the Mass is, of course, our reception of Jesus in Holy Communion. We should make the most of these special moments. Let's properly thank Jesus for coming to us with His Body, Blood, Soul, and Divinity. Let's thank Jesus for the tremendous suffering He experienced to be able to give us the Eucharist. As Jesus dwells within us, in this precious way at communion time, we should tell Him how much we love Him. At communion time, the very Heart of Christ—this Heart which is a symbol of His great love for His Father and for us—dwells within us. This Heart cries out for our love in return. Should we not tell Jesus?:

> O Jesus, I do love You so much! Help me grow in love for You! Help me to grow in the realization of the great love with which Your Heart beat for me upon Calvary, a love which is present in Your glorified Heart, here and now. Let me grasp, with deeper knowledge, that Your Heart was pierced on Calvary with a soldier's lance for love of me! Take me, Jesus,

ever more closely to Your Heart. And there, let me draw from this burning furnace of charity. Thus, strengthened, refreshed, and encouraged, let me go forth to live the Mass all day, every day.

One of the great means God has given us to help us prepare ourselves for better participation in the Mass is the Sacrament of Reconciliation. Our Lady of Medjugorje asks us to go to confession at least once a month. She had also requested it at Fatima through the first Saturday message.

Indeed, we should use all available means to prepare ourselves for a more fruitful participation in the Eucharistic Sacrifice. It is a great privilege to be able to be present at, and to participate in, the Mass. We should show Jesus our appreciation for such a great gift by preparing ourselves as best we can, and in this way we will gain the greatest possible benefit from the Mass, both for ourselves and for others.

Read, again, the prayer given to the three children at Fatima, a most profound message regarding the importance of the Eucharist and the true Presence:

> *Most Holy Trinity, Father, Son and Holy Spirit, I adore You profoundly. I offer You the most precious Body, Blood, Soul, and Divinity of Jesus Christ, present in all tabernacles of the world, in reparation for the outrages, sacrileges, and indifference by which He is offended. By the infinite merits of the Sacred Heart of Jesus and* [the intercession of] *the Immaculate Heart of Mary, I beg of Thee the conversion of poor sinners.*

thirteen

Prayer

There is no word which Our Lady of Medjugorje uses more often than the word **pray**. In her messages, Mary is incessantly pleading with us to pray, pray, pray! When the visionaries, Vicka and Ivan, spoke to us at Medjugorje, they emphasized Mary's great stress on prayer.

The following are some of the many passages in which our Blessed Mother speaks to us about prayer:

Dear children, today like never before, I invite you to prayer. Your prayer should be a prayer for peace. Satan is strong and wishes not only to destroy human life but also nature and the planet on which you live. Therefore, dear children, pray that you can protect yourselves through prayer with the blessings of God's peace. God sent me to you so that I can help you. If you wish to, grasp the Rosary. The Rosary alone can do miracles in the world and in your lives... (January 25, 1991).

Dear children, I call you to prayer. By means of prayer, little children, you obtain joy and peace. Through prayer, you are richer in the mercy of God. Therefore, little children, let prayer be the life of each one of you. Especially,

I call you to pray so that all those who are far away from God may be converted... (August 25, 1988).

Dear children, you are a chosen people, and God has given you great graces. You are not aware of every message I am giving you. Now I only wish to say—pray, pray, pray! I do not know what else to tell you because I love you and wish that, in prayer, you come to know my love and the love of God (November 15, 1984).

That prayer and reparation is vital for the conversion of the world was also specifically stated at Fatima. During one of the apparitions the children were told:

Pray! Pray a great deal. The Hearts of Jesus and Mary have merciful designs on you. Offer prayers and sacrifices continually to the Most High. Make everything you do a sacrifice, and offer it as an act of reparation for the sins by which God is offended and as a petition for the conversion of sinners.

In the second of the above messages, Mary tells us, "...let prayer be the life of each one of you." Indeed, our Mother is telling us how much we should esteem prayer. How well she knows that we can't accomplish God's plan for us unless we pray! And being the perfect Mother, she offers to help us pray. In the first of the above messages, Mary says, "God sent me to you so that I can help you." Mary helps us in all aspects of our spiritual lives, prayer included.

Mary is eager to be our companion in prayer. When Mary walked this earth, she was aglow with love for God and for all of God's children. Mary's prayer was permeated with a depth of love we are unable to comprehend fully. We should constantly ask her to obtain for us the grace to make our prayer more deeply centered in love for God and neighbor. Jesus has summed up His religion in terms of love. He has told us to love God with our whole being and our neighbor as ourselves (*Matt.* 22:37-40). Prayer helps to thrust us foward to a greater expression of love for God and neighbor. In the quiet of prayer, we must allow the fire of love to more fully possess us so that we come to realize right down to the depths of our being that to truly live is to love. Mary, in showing us her Heart as symbol of her love for God and us, vividly reminds us of this truth.

Love of God is inseparable from a desire to do His will. Here again, Mary is our teacher. In her prayer, Our Lady was consumed to do God's will in all things. Her words in the Gospel perfectly sum up her life. Behold Mary at the Annunciation: *" 'I am the handmaid of the Lord,' said Mary, 'let what you have said be done to me.' And the angel left her"* (*Luke* 1:38). In prayer, we too must find the inspiration and strength to do God's will. In prayer, we must grow in the desire to be open to whatever God asks of us, whether this be easy or difficult.

Mary was Jesus' first and perfect disciple. Everything in her life was in some way connected with Christ. Her prayer life was supremely Christocentric. Being Christ's Mother and perfect follower, she is admirably suited to teach us how to put Christ at the center of our prayer.

Discussing prayer leads us to say a few words about the Rosary. The Rosary is very obviously centered in Christ. As we pray the Rosary, Mary leads us to a prayerful reflection on the life, passion, death, and resurrection of Jesus. Pope Paul VI tells us:

As a Gospel prayer, centered on the mystery
of the redemptive Incarnation, the Rosary is,
therefore, a prayer with a clearly Christological
orientation....The Jesus that each Hail Mary
recalls is the same Jesus Whom the succession
of the mysteries preposes to us.[49]

At Fatima, Mary identified herself as "The Lady of the
Rosary." She specifically asked that the Rosary be prayed
every day. At Medjugorje, she has often repeated this
request:

*Say every day, at least one Rosary—Joyful,
Sorrowful, and Glorious Mysteries* (August 14,
1984).

Besides the Rosary, there are other methods of prayer
we can use. Closely associated with the Rosary is the
method of meditation whereby we choose a scene, an
event, from Christ's life for prayerful consideration.
Using this method, we observe the persons involved in
the Gospel scene. We consider their words and their
actions. As we do this, we make application to our own
Christian existence.

Another excellent way to pray is to take up the Bible,
read a short passage, and prayerfully reflect on it. Then
the process can be repeated with another passage. However, one should remain with one particular passage as
long as one feels drawn to do so. There is no need to
rush on. One may wish to remain with just one passage
for the entire prayer period.

Simple conversation with God, about anything and
everthing, is another way of praying. We should feel at
ease discussing all aspects of our life with God.

The Mass, of course, is the most excellent form of

prayer. As Christ's sacrifice on Calvary is made truly present at each Eucharistic sacrifice, we pray together, with Christ, to the Father, in the Holy Spirit, and in union with Mary. Christ, Chief Priest and Victim in the Mass, unites our gift of ourselves to His own self-giving. We offer in the spirit of adoration, thanksgiving, petition, and reparation for sin.

Whenever we have the reasonable opportunity, we should pray before the Blessed Sacrament. Jesus, our perfect Friend, is really present in the tabernacle—Body, Blood, Soul, and Divinity. What a tremendous and unfathomable gift Jesus gives us in His Eucharistic presence!

As previously stated, Eucharistic reparation and adoration of the Blessed Sacrament were strongly encouraged at Fatima, through the prayers taught to the children by the Angel. They are detailed in the first part of this book. Our Lady confirms this most urgent need at Medjugorje, as well. On March 15, 1984, she stated:

Adore continually the Most Holy Sacrament. I am always present when the faithful are in adoration. Special graces are then being received.

Why is there so much neglect and indifference shown to Jesus in His Eucharistic presence? How many there are who no longer believe in His real presence! How many there are, who, although believing, have little or no interest in visiting Jesus, present in the Blessed Sacrament! One aspect of our own prayer before the Blessed Sacrament should be a spirit of reparation, which helps atone for the coldness, indifference, and sacrileges committed against Jesus, really present in the Eucharist. We repeat here, again, the prayer given by the Angel to the three young Fatima visionaries:

> *Most Holy Trinity, Father, Son and Holy*
> *Spirit, I adore You profoundly. I offer You the*
> *most precious Body, Blood, Soul, and Divinity*
> *of Jesus Christ, present in all tabernacles of the*
> *world, in reparation for the outrages, sacrileges,*
> *and indifference by which He is offended. By*
> *the infinite merits of the Sacred Heart of Jesus*
> *and* [the intercession of] *the Immaculate Heart*
> *of Mary, I beg of Thee the conversion of poor*
> *sinners.* [50]

Let's pray, pray, pray—as Our Lady of Medjugorje asks us. With God's help, let's resolve not to give in to discouragement when we find it difficult to pray. Let's determine not to yield to the temptation which tells us we are too busy to pray (what a monumental falsehood this is!). Let's determine not to yield to the temptation which suggests that, rather than pray, we can better serve God and neighbor in other ways. Yes, we must serve God and neighbor in a variety of ways, but the time which should be reserved for prayer must never be neglected.

It is impossible to live out properly our consecration to the Hearts of Jesus and Mary without a consistent prayer life. In our act of consecration, we give ourselves entirely to Jesus and Mary—our entire selves and all our good deeds. In this consecration, we promise to try to conform to the will of God in all things, every day.

Yes, our consecration is a total gift of self. We entrust this total gift of ourselves to Mary the Immaculate Heart—what a perfect and beautiful way to give ourselves to the Heart of Jesus!

Is there anyone who thinks we can make and live such

a total offering of ourselves without a consistent prayer life? We need not fear, though, regarding the great challenge our consecration presents to us. Mary, the one Jesus has given to us as our Mother, is ever at our side to help us with her tender, loving, maternal care. Remember what she tells us in the message which begins this chapter: *"God sent me to you so that I can help you."*

fourteen

Fasting and Other Forms of the Cross

I ask the people to pray with me these days. Pray all the more. Fast strictly on Wednesday and Friday. Say, every day, at least one Rosary: Joyful, Sorrowful, and Glorious Mysteries (August 14, 1984).

Dear children! For these days when you celebrate the Cross with joy, I wish your cross to be joyful. Dear children, pray that you can accept sickness and suffering with love, like Jesus. Only in that way can I give you, with joy, the graces of healing that Jesus allows. Thank you for your response to my call (September 11, 1986).

Dear children! I wish to tell you to put the Cross at the center of your life. Pray, especially before the Cross from which great graces are coming. Now, in your homes, make a special consecration to the Cross of the Lord. Promise that you will not offend Jesus and that you will not insult Him. Thank you for your response to my call (September 12, 1985).

Fasting and sacrifice also became daily regime for the children of Fatima. Reparation for the sins of mankind

100

was extremely important to them, for Our Lady had told them:

> *Pray, pray a great deal, and make many sacrifices, for many souls go to Hell because they have no one to make sacrifices and to pray for them.*

In the above messages, Mary speaks to us about the Cross. She is reminding us of the central place the Cross has in Jesus' teaching:

> *Then to all He said, "If anyone wants to be a follower of mine, let him renounce himself and take up his cross every day and follow me. For anyone who wants to save his life will lose it; but anyone who loses his life for my sake, that man will save it"* (*Luke* 9:23-24).

It is very important to notice that, in this Scripture passage, Jesus makes the connection between the cross and life. He tells us that we can't have true life without the cross. This follows the pattern of His own life. By dying on the Cross, Jesus entered into the glory of His resurrection and gave us life. His Cross was the way to the life of resurrection for Himself and for us. The more we share His Cross—the more we mystically die with Him out of love—the more we share His life of resurrection, here and hereafter. And very importantly, we should realize that the cross does not mean a lack of joy in our lives. In the second of the Medjugorje messages quoted above, Mary reminds us that we should incorporate the cross into our lives in a spirit of joy. Actually, the more we die with Jesus—the more we carry our cross with Him—the more we experience true joy. Why? Because the more we mystically die with Jesus in the carrying of the cross, the more united with Him we become, and the more united we are with Jesus, the more we share in the joy of His resurrection.

All the saints are outstanding examples of following in their Master's footsteps. They walked the way of Calvary. They profoundly shared in the suffering of Christ and profoundly shared in His resurrection—the newness of life—here and hereafter. Consumed with a great love for God and neighbor, they were great witnesses to the words of St. Paul:

> "...we carry with us in our body the death of Jesus, so that the life of Jesus, too, may always be seen in our body. Indeed, while we are still alive, we are consigned to our death every day, for the sake of Jesus, so that in our mortal flesh the life of Jesus, too, may be openly shown" (*2 Cor.* 4:10-11).

What a beautiful expression of our sharing in the death-resurrection of Jesus!

In the first of Our Lady's messages quoted above, she mentions fasting as one of the forms of the cross she wants us to embrace. If it is possible, she asks that we fast on bread and water on Wednesdays and Fridays. Fasting can take many other forms. It is simply denying ourselves of some earthly desire or perceived need.

Fasting is not the only form of the cross Mary speaks about. She talks about the general role which sacrifice plays in our Christian lives. She continually stresses it at Medjugorje, and it was a major emphasis in the lives of the Fatima children.

The cross is present in our lives in many ways. A primary source for our participation in the Cross of Jesus is the effort required to be faithful to our daily duties. In the performance of these duties, we invariably have to endure little crosses—and sometimes big ones. Failure, loneliness, sickness, injury, rejection, being misunderstood, feeling unappreciated, renunciation, and the effort of self-discipline—these also are common forms of the cross. We could extend the list further.

However the cross is present in our lives, we should daily ask for the grace not to waste suffering. The great tragedy concerning human suffering is not that there is so much of it, but that apparently so much of it is wasted. When a person wastes suffering—does not relate to it according to God's will—then that suffering is not life-producing. In God's plan, suffering is meant to lead to greater life—here and hereafter. If we use suffering properly, if we truly die with Christ, then we grow as Christians. We grow in the life Jesus came to give us in abundance, and we become more apt instruments for helping to channel this life to others. Summarily, the more we die with Christ, the more we rise with Christ. Here again, the messages of Fatima and Medjugorje are identical.

He hung upon a Cross on a hill called Calvary. Before being mercilessly nailed to the Cross, He had been brutally scourged and crowned with thorns. The long climb with the Cross further weakened our loving Savior. Now, He hung there. His lacerated and most holy Body was covered with His precious Blood. At the foot of the Cross, there valiantly stood Mary, Mother of Jesus and our Mother. Her great suffering was second only to that of her Son. Who can prayerfully look upon this magnificent pair—Jesus and Mary—and not be deeply moved? Jesus and Mary suffered so much for us! They show us

Their Hearts as symbols of Their love for us. In our Act of Consecration to the Hearts of Jesus and Mary, we say with our entire being that, yes, we do want to give our love to Jesus and Mary. In the daily living out of our consecration, the bearing of the cross is inevitable. Assisted by Jesus and Mary, we do not shirk the challenge. We are continually motivated to a greater love, ever mindful of that terrible but poignantly beautiful scene on Calvary, where the love of Jesus, aided by Mary's cooperation with Jesus and the Will of God, redeemed us from our sins and made possible for us the fullness of life, in Christ Jesus, Our Lord.

fifteen

The Reading of Scripture

Scripture is one of our great sources for growth in the knowledge and love of Christ. Mary knows this much better than we do, and so at Medjugorje she has explicitly reminded us of the importance of Scripture reading for our life in Christ. The prayerful reading of the Bible, especially the Gospels, is a mighty help given us for our growth in our life of consecration to God. The gift we make of ourselves to the Hearts of Jesus and Mary becomes all the more pure, noble, and loving the more we take in, and live by, the wisdom which the pages of Scripture offer us.

At Medjugorje our Blessed Mother tells us:

> *Dear children! Today I ask you to read the Bible in your homes every day, and let it be in a visible place there, so that it always encourages you to read and pray* (October 18, 1984).

> *. . . Every family must pray family prayer and read the Bible* (February 14, 1985).

Some say, "I don't have time in my busy schedule to read the Bible every day." If a person thinks this way, that person has a misguided set of priorities. We always find the time for that which we consider important. If we think reading the Bible is important—and no true Christian denies that it is—then we will find the time to read Scripture daily. There is more than one way to find time if we really want to—for instance, by turning off the TV set. Here again, Mary has words of wisdom for us, her children:

> *Dear children, this Lent is a special incentive for you to change. Start from this moment. Turn off the television, and renounce various things that are of no value. Dear children, I am calling you individually to conversion. This season is for you* (February 13, 1986).

We really need to pray for a deeper appreciation of the worth of Scripture for our Christian lives. The Bible is one of God's greatest gifts to us. Shouldn't we strive to grow in the realization of this? And shouldn't our growth in this realization logically lead us to read Scripture consistently and pray for the grace to incorporate its wisdom and its power into our daily lives?

sixteen

Peace

During our pilgrimage group's meetings with the visionaries, Ivan and Vicka, at Medjugorje, we heard both of them stress the important role which peace has in Mary's teaching. Here are some of Our Lady's messages which speak to us of peace.

Dear children! Without prayer, there is no peace. Therefore, I say to you, pray at the foot of the Cross for peace (September 6, 1984).

Dear children, today I thank you and want to invite you all to God's peace. I want to invite you to experience in your heart that peace which God gives. Today I want to bless all of you. I bless you with God's blessing. I beg you, dear children, to follow and to live my way (June 25, 1987).

St. Augustine tells us in his classic work, *The City of God,* that peace is the tranquility of order. God is the ultimate Giver of order. God has put a plan—a certain order—in His work of creation. To the extent that the human race respects this plan of God, peace exists among the members of the human family. To the extent that humans do not respect God's plan, by variously going against His will, peace is lacking in the world.

We see, then, that it is no accident that there is such a lack of peace in today's world—lack of peace between nations, within nations, within many families, and within the Church. Because God's will, in so many instances, is being seriously violated by sin of all kinds, we have a critical lack of peace in today's world. We are experiencing such a radical lack of true peace because God's plan or order is so blatantly disregarded. Remember, peace is the tranquility of order.

At Fatima, we were specifically given the "conditions for peace." The prophecies given by Our Lady also outlined the consequences if mankind did not respond. The same requests have been made by Our Lady at Medjugorje, for years, and we can now once again see the results of mankind's stubbornness.

The more we individually progress in our own loving conformity to God's will, the more peace we experience in our hearts. In the first of the above quoted messages, Mary points out the necessity of prayer for growth in peace. She is telling us that we need the inspiration and strength of prayer to increasingly conform ourselves, in love, to the Father's will.

Our Lady also reminds us that the more we grow in God's peace, the more apt instruments we become for spreading peace in the world. She tells us:

> *Dear children, through your own peace, I am calling you to help others to see and to start searching for peace. Dear children, you are at peace, and therefore, you cannot comprehend the absence of peace. Again, I am calling you so that, through prayer and your life, you will help destroy everything evil in people and uncover the deception which Satan is using.*

Pray for truth to prevail in every heart (September 23, 1986).

Connecting our pursuit of peace with our consecration to the Hearts of Jesus and Mary, we can say that the more deeply we live out this consecration, the more peace we personally experience. Why? This peace comes about because growth in our consecration means we are more fully surrendering ourselves to the Heart of Christ, through the Immaculate Heart of Mary. And increased surrender to Jesus means we are allowing Him to take us closer to the Father, in the Spirit, through a deepened, loving conformity to the Father's will. Growth in peace, in turn, results from this evolving union with God's will. Peace is the tranquility of order. It is the peace resulting from doing God's will—this will which is the ultimate source of all true order.

seventeen

On Giving Thanks

Dear children! These days the Lord has granted you many graces. Let this week be a week of thanksgiving for all the graces God has granted you... (January 3, 1985).

Dear children, today I invite you all to rejoice in the life which God gives you. Little children, rejoice in God the Creator because He has created you so wonderfully. Pray that your life may be full of joy and thanksgiving, which flows out of your heart like a river of joy. Little children, give thanks unceasingly for all that you possess and for each little gift that God has given you so that a joyful blessing always comes down from God upon your life... (August 25, 1988).

Our consecration to the Father, Son, and Holy Spirit, lived out in the Hearts of Jesus and Mary, requires that we constantly give thanks to God. Mary reminds us of this in the above messages. Jesus, Himself, has taught us that we must always be thankful. In the Gospel scene which describes how Jesus cleansed the ten lepers, we have these words:

Finding himself cured, one of them turned back, praising God at the top of his voice, and

110

threw himself at the feet of Jesus and thanked Him. The man was a Samaritan. This made Jesus say, "Were not all ten made clean? The other nine, where are they? It seems that no one has come back to give praise to God, except this foreigner" (*Luke* 17:15-18).

Each one of us has to ask, "Do I belong to the group of nine lepers who did not give thanks? Or do I stand beside the one leper who gave proper thanks to God?"

eighteen

Joy and Happiness

Dear children, I am inviting you to a complete surrender to God. Pray, little children, that Satan may not carry you about like branches in the wind. Be strong in God. I desire that, through you, the whole world may get to know the God of joy. By your life, bear witness for God's joy. Do not be anxious nor worried. God Himself will help you and show you the way. I desire that you love all mankind with my love. Only in that way can love reign over the world. . . (May 25, 1988).

Dear children: Today I would like to envelop you with my mantle and lead you toward the road to resurrection. Dear children, I beg you to give Our Lord your past and all the evil that has accumulated in your hearts. I want all of you to be happy, and with sin, no one can be happy. That is why, dear children, you must pray, and in your prayers you will realize the path to happiness. Happiness will be in your heart and you will be the witness to that which I and my Son want for all of you (February 25, 1987).

All people desire to experience joy and happiness. Sadly, so many seek joy and happiness in the wrong way.

This has been true at all times of human history. This is the situation today more than ever. Our Lady has told us that the world is afflicted by an unprecedented wave of sinfulness. She is begging the world to turn from the wrong ways of seeking joy and happiness and to convert to God. She is telling us that to pursue joy and happiness away from God is actually to pursue joylessness and unhappiness. No real joy and happiness is possible apart from God. Again, it is a mirror image of the events at Fatima.

Sorrow, suffering, anxieties of various sorts—these are all part of life within the human condition. Yet, if amidst all of this we are not basically joyful and happy people, something is amiss. The Christian vocation includes the call to be joyful. If we live properly in Christ Jesus, we will share His joy despite the painful dimension of being human. Jesus tells us:

> *I have told you this so that my own joy may*
> *be in you and your joy be complete* (*John*
> 15:11).

Western, industrialized culture has tended to create the illusion that joy can be bought and that, the more money one has, the greater are a person's prospects of enjoying life. This tragic illusion has time and again prevented people from living in a manner which alone can give true joy. We must pray for the light and strength not to be entrapped by this insidious view of our times.

Even if we consider ourselves to be basically good Christians, we can miss opportunities for experiencing true joy if we do not keep our Christian perspective finely honed. There are ongoing occasions every day for experiencing joy—each moment provides them. But we can often pass them by, unaware of their joy-producing possibilities, because we have foolishly narrowed our expectations regarding what is a source of joy and happiness and what is not.

Real and lasting joy and happiness come only when we are willing to cooperate with God's grace and live a deep spiritual life. Only then will we experience the substantial joy and happiness we all desire. It is such a life that Our Lady of Medjugorje is calling us to live through her messages. To put it in terms of consecration—the underlying and summary teaching of Fatima and Medjugorje—we increase our joy and happiness to the degree that we live out our consecration to the Hearts of Jesus and Mary.

In the above quoted messages, our Mother reminds us that the way of life she proposes to us at Medjugorje—the way of consecration—is the only way to experience true joy and happiness. In one of the above passages, she tells us: *"I want all of you to be happy, and with sin, no one can be happy. That is why, dear children, you must pray, and in your prayers you will realize the path to happiness."* At Fatima, she had stated as much, also telling us that war is the result of sin. Mankind's actions continue to prove her correct.

Mary is the wisest of Mothers. She wants to lead us to a joy and happiness which is always on the increase. Our joy and happiness take root within us at an ever deeper level the more we live out our consecration to the Hearts of Jesus and Mary. She speaks about surrendering ourselves to her—this is consecration to her Immaculate Heart—so that she can lead us ever closer to God, the source of all joy and happiness. She tells us: *"I love you and I want you to surrender to me so that I can lead you to God. . . . Pray for the knowledge that you are mine. I bless you with blessings of joy."*

nineteen

Surrender to God

Dear children! Open your hearts to the Holy Spirit in a special way these days. The Holy Spirit is working in a special way through you. Open your hearts and give your lives to Jesus so that He will work through your hearts and strengthen you (May 23, 1985).

Dear children! Today I am calling you to live and to pay attention, with a special love, to all the messages which I am giving you. God does not want you lukewarm and indecisive, but totally committed to Him. You know that I love you and that I am burning out of love for you. Therefore, dear children, commit yourselves to love so that you will comprehend and burn with God's love from day to day. Decide for love, dear children, so that love may prevail in all of you—not human love, but God's love. Thank you for your response to my call (November 20, 1986).

In the above messages, Our Blessed Mother speaks of surrender to God. Mary reminds us that we are called to complete and total surrender to God.

Growth in our consecration to the Heart of Christ and to the Immaculate Heart means an ever greater surrender

115

or abandonment to Jesus and Mary. As we increasingly entrust ourselves to the Heart of our Mother, she increasingly gives us the desire to grow in the depth of our gift of self—our surrender—to the Heart of Jesus. As we grow in our assimilation to Christ, He leads us ever closer to the Father, in the Holy Spirit.

Abandonment or surrender to God is associated with the idea of spiritual childhood. Notice how Mary consistently introduces her messages with the salutation *"Dear children"* and how often she calls us *"little children."* She wants us to remember what her Son, Jesus, has told us:

> At this time the disciples came to Jesus and said, "Who is the greatest in the kingdom of heaven?" So He called a little child to Him and set the child in front of them. Then He said, "I tell you solemnly, unless you change and become like little children, you will never enter the Kingdom of Heaven. And so, the one who makes himself as little as this little child is the greatest in the Kingdom of Heaven" (*Matt.* 18:1-4).

Jesus and Mary don't want us to be **childish.** They want us to be **childlike.** One of the greatest characteristics of little children is their very pronounced dependence on their parents. They look to their parents for their various needs. They trust their parents. They feel that, no matter what happens, their parents will take care of them. Children, by nature, have a sense of surrender to the care of their parents.

When Jesus and Mary refer to us as children, they are striving to deepen within us the realization that we are totally dependent on God. Without God, we are helpless. Growth in the spiritual life is proportionate to the deepened sense of our helplessness and the accompanying increase in surrender to God. And, in one of the many paradoxes of the Christian life, the more we realize our helplessness and the more we throw ourselves into the arms of Jesus and Mary, the stronger we become. St. Paul says:

> *So I shall be very happy to make my weaknesses my special boast so that the power of Christ may stay over me, and that is why I am quite content with my weaknesses, and with insults, hardships, persecutions, and the agonies I go through for Christ's sake. For it is when I am weak that I am strong (2 Cor. 12:9-10).*

The most difficult challenge facing us in the spiritual life is giving up the sense of control over our lives and surrendering ourselves more and more to the control of Jesus. We have to realize that, in our Act of Consecration to the Heart of Christ, we are telling Jesus we are giving ourselves completely to Him. We are telling Him, "Jesus, I want to allow You to control my life completely." To do this day after day takes an unusual spiritual determination. We must constantly pray for this special grace. Jesus, in words to one of His chosen ones, reminds us of the need for this self-surrender to Him:

> *My people need to surrender their control to me. I will then be able to fill them with my radiance. This also is part of obedience. The most difficult thing for my people to do is to give me their control! They are afraid they will lose their power. How can I express the seriousness of this lesson on control?*

By trying to hold onto power, they will lose it, because they are grasping the wrong source of power. By surrendering your control, you shall gain it because you shall be gaining my control! Being afraid of following my ways because of the need to surrender control is an emotion placed in you by the evil one!

So trust in me when I say to surrender unto me with an open heart. You will gain control...my control...and you shall never fear again. You will only be filled with my goodness, my happiness, my mercy, my power, my love, and my peace![51]

twenty

A Deep Spirituality

Dear children, today I am calling you to complete surrender to God. Everything you do and everything you possess give over to God so that He can take control in your life as the King of all that you possess. That way, through me, God can lead you into the depths of the spiritual life... (July 25, 1988).

Dear children, today I am blessing you in a special way with my motherly blessing, and I am interceding for you before God, that He will give you the gift of conversion of the heart. For years, I am calling you and exhorting you to a deep spiritual life and simplicity (December 25, 1989).

In the above passages, Mary speaks about the deep spirituality contained in the Medjugorje messages. In other messages, our Mother talks about our complete conversion to God, our complete surrender to Him, a life full of holiness. Whether she is using these particular phrases or words speaking of a deep spiritual life, she is talking about the same reality. Our Mother is calling us to the heights of sanctity! She is calling us to a complete—to a fully developed—living of our baptismal consecration. She is calling us to a complete development of the life of holiness we receive in Baptism.

As we said previously, in this, our age, Jesus and Mary are calling us to live out and develop our baptismal consecration through consecration to their Hearts.

The Medjugorje call to a deep spiritual life—a life of complete conversion, a complete surrender to God—is a call to a complete surrender to the Sacred Heart and to the Immaculate Heart. Giving ourselves, our lives, all our faculties, all our good deeds—everything—to the Hearts of Jesus and Mary is the life Our Lady of Medjugorje calls us to. To the degree that we answer her call, she uses our lives to help bring the world back to God.

There is no need to fear this call to the heights of sanctity. Responding to the great love of the Heart of Jesus, and to the maternal love of the Heart of Mary, we abandon ourselves to our Savior and to our Mother. We rest secure within the refuge of the Hearts of Jesus and Mary, strengthened for the ongoing battle being waged with Their adversary, Satan.

Mary's call to a deep spiritual life is a call to the joy and the happiness we all desire in the fullest measure. Every day we should pray to Jesus and Mary that They may draw us closer to Their Hearts. Within the refuge of Their Hearts, we grow in sanctity. Through the Heart of Mary, we hand ourselves over to the Heart of Christ with an ever deeper love, so that He can lead us closer to the bosom of the Father, in the Holy Spirit.

twenty-one

Angels

Angels have often been involved in the Medjugorje apparitions of Our Lady. Mary is reminding us of their important role in salvation history, encouraging us to honor them and to call upon their intercession. Angels are prominent throughout the Bible—in both the Old and New Testaments. They are special messengers in God's plan. Let us again make the connection between Fatima and Medjugorje.

It was an Angel who first appeared to the children at Fatima. It was the Angel who gave us the very important Fatima prayers. He asked the children to pray with him the following prayer:

> *My God, I believe, I adore, I trust and I love Thee. I ask pardon for those who do not believe, do not adore, do not trust, and do not love Thee!*

It is interesting to note that Mary also stresses the importance of devotion to the angels in her communications with Fr. Gobbi, spiritual director of the Marian Movement of Priests. Through Fr. Gobbi, she tells us that it is especially important to entrust ourselves to the angels at this particular stage of history, when the influence of Satan and his followers is so strong.[52]

We should have special devotion to the Archangels

121

Michael, Gabriel, and Raphael, and to our own guardian angel. Besides our own way of praying to the angels, we should also use two classic prayers, one to St. Michael and the other to our own particular Guardian Angel. The prayer to St. Michael was composed by Pope Leo XIII after he received a vision in which he was shown the battle that would be waged between Satan and St. Michael over the Church. The battle is now at its fiercest. We should say this prayer each day:

> St. Michael the Archangel, defend us in the day of battle. Be our safeguard against the wickedness and snares of the devil. May God rebuke him, we humbly pray, and do thou, O Prince of the Heavenly Host, by the power of God, cast into Hell, Satan, and all the other evil spirits, who prowl through the world, seeking the ruin of souls. Amen.[53]

And here is the prayer to our individual guardian angel. As we say it each day, let's pray for the grace to realize how great and loyal a friend our guardian angels are. Let's pray for the grace to realize the great role our angels play in our lives.

> Angel of God, my guardian dear, to whom God's love commits me here; ever this day be at my side, to light and guard, to rule and guide. Amen.[54]

twenty-two

Our Personal Call and Role

Dear children! Today again, I want to call you to begin to live the new life from today onward. Dear children, I want you to comprehend that God has chosen each one of you in order to use you for the great plan of salvation of mankind. You cannot comprehend how great your role is in God's plan. Therefore, dear children, pray so that, through prayer, you may comprehend God's plan toward you. I am with you so that you can realize it completely (January 25, 1987).

Once again our Mother tells us that God has great plans for us for the salvation of mankind. She asks us to pray so that we may receive the light to understand God's role for us.

It is a repetition of her requests made at Fatima—requests that, if heeded, would have spared mankind decades of misery. Her call in 1917 centered on conversion, reparation, penance, prayer, ingredients of total consecration. They specified our individual participation in helping to save souls from Hell and aiding in the conversion of sinners.

Medjugorje parallels these same messages, and her appearances there have evolved into a "school of holiness," a blueprint for our ongoing sanctification and our ultimate salvation.

What is our response to God's call, which He gives to us through Mary? Do we realize the preciousness of each moment of our existence? Each moment is a God-given opportunity to love Him and our neighbor. Each moment of our lives is an opportunity to contribute positively to the dramatic struggle being waged between Our Lady and her adversary, Satan.

What has been our response to the call which God and Mary put before us? What is our response now? What is going to be our response in the future?

Each of us has a mission to fulfill in life. I can't fulfill yours; you can't fulfill mine. Cardinal Newman reminds us:

> Everyone who breathes, high and low, edu-
> cated and ignorant, young and old, man and
> woman, has a mission, has a work. We are not
> sent into this world for nothing; we are not born
> at random....God sees every one of us; He
> creates every soul, He lodges it in a body, one
> by one, for a purpose.[55]

Each day, as we determine to live anew our consecration to the Hearts of Jesus and Mary, we are fulfilling our mission in life. We are helping Jesus and Mary in the work of ongoing redemption. We have to fight the temptation which says that we are of little value, that what we do or don't do doesn't much matter. This is not the way Jesus and Mary look upon our lives. They see the preciousness of each individual. They see the greatness of our daily lives when these lives are lived out in loving conformity to God's will.

We are great because God has made us great. Without God we are nothing. Without Him we are completely helpless. But when we live in union with God, we allow our God-given greatness to increasingly emerge, and we accomplish marvels, the marvels of His will, of His plan for us—the salvation of our souls, and our prayers and sacrifices for the souls of others.

Each day is a new and glorious opportunity to say "yes" to God's plan for us. We should pray each day for the light and strength to say "yes." We should pray to realize, in an ever deeper fashion, that no one can say "yes" for us, that no one can fulfill the roles God has assigned to each of us.

To have a role which no one else can fulfill is an awesome privilege and responsibility. There is no reason to feel overwhelmed, however, for we have the source for success. Resting secure within the refuge of the Hearts of Jesus and Mary, we find the love, peace, security, and strength we need to fulfill our tasks.

Notes

1. For background material on Fatima, I am particularly indebted to *Our Lady of Fatima's Peace Plan from Heaven* (Rockford: TAN Books and Publishers, Inc., 1983).
2. *Ibid.,* pp. 7-8.
3. Louis Kondar, SVD, editor, *Fatima in Lucia's Own Words* (Fatima: Postulation Center, 1976), p. 62. Distributed in the U.S.A. by the Ravengate Press, Cambridge, MA.
4. *Our Lady's Peace Plan, op. cit.,* pp. 1-2.
5. *Ibid.,* p. 2 (The words in brackets are my own—added for clarification).
6. *Fatima in Lucia's Own Words, op. cit.,* pp. 64-65.
7. Frere Michael de la Trinité, *The Whole Truth about Fatima* (Buffalo: Immaculate Heart Publications, 1989), pp. 85-86 (The words in brackets are my own—added for clarification).
8. *Ibid.,* pp. 112-114.
9. *Our Lady's Peace Plan, op. cit.,* p. 30.
10. *Ibid.,* p. 3.
11. *Ibid.,* pp. 3-4.
12. *Ibid.,* pp. 4-5.
13. *Ibid.,* p. 5.
14. Rev. Edward Carter, S.J., *Mother at Our Side: Mary's Role in the Spiritual Life* (1993: Faith Publishing Co., Milford, Ohio), p. 21.
15. *Our Lady's Peace Plan, op. cit.,* p. 6.
16. *Ibid.,* p. 6.
17. *Ibid.,* p. 7.
18. *Ibid.,* p. 8.
19. *Ibid.,* pp. 9-10.
20. Pope John-Paul II, as quoted in Arthur Collin, *Totus Tuus:*

John Paul's Program of Marian Consecration and Entrustment (Libertyville: Academy of the Immaculate, 1992), p. 177.

21. René Laurentin, as quoted in *Queen of Peace,* Pittsburgh Center for Peace, Winter, 1993, p. 11.
22. *The Whole Truth about Fatima, op. cit.,* p. 182.
23. The Medjugorje messages through 1991 are taken from David Golob's *Live the Messages* (Harahan, Louisiana, Box 23351, 1991). Also available from The Riehle Foundation, P.O. Box 7, Milford, Ohio 45150.

     Messages after 1991 are taken from the "Blue Letter," published by The Riehle Foundation, Milford, Ohio, and from *A Call to Peace,* published at Bella Vista, Arkansas.
24. *Our Lady's Peace Plan, op. cit.,* p. 10.
25. Archbishop R. Arulappa, *The Two Hearts,* in *The Fatima Crusader,* Summer, 1992, p. 3.
26. *Our Lady's Peace Plan, op. cit.,* p. 14.
27. *To the Priests, Our Lady's Beloved Sons* (St. Francis: The Marian Movement of Priests, 12th English edition, 1991), Nos. 287 and 425. This book, which contains Mary's messages or locutions to Don (Fr.) Stefano Gobbi, may be obtained free of charge, although voluntary contributions allow its free distribution. In the U.S.A. English, French, Spanish, and Italian copies may be obtained by writing to:

The Marian Movement of Priests
P.O. Box 8
St. Francis, Maine 04774-0008

In Canada, copies (English only) may be obtained by writing to:

The Marian Movement of Priests
1515 Bathurst Street
Toronto, Ontario M5P 3H4

28. A. Bossard, in *Dictionary of Mary* (New York: Catholic Book Publishing Co., 1985), pp. 54-55.
29. *Ibid.,* p. 55.
30. Pope John Paul II, *The Mother of the Redeemer (Redemptoris Mater)* (Washington: United States Catholic Conference, 1987), No. 45.
31. *Totus Tuus, op. cit.,* p. 63.
32. St. Louis de Montfort, *God Alone: The Collected Writings of St. Louis de Montfort* (Bay Shore: Montfort Publications, 1987), p. 327.
33. *Our Lady's Peace Plan, op. cit.,* p. 23.
34. Pope John Paul II, as quoted in *Totus Tuus, op. cit.,* p. 255.
35. *Bonaventure,* translated by Evert Collins (New York: Paulist Press, 1978), pp. 154-155.
36. Pope Pius XII, *Haurietis Aquas* (New York: Paulist Press, 1956), No. 119.
37. *Ibid.,* No. 65.
38. *The Letters of St. Margaret Mary Alacoque,* translated by Clarence A. Herbst, S.J. (Chicago: Henry Regnery Company, 1954), pp. 37-38.
39. Pope Pius XII, *Haurietis Aquas, op. cit.,* Nos. 92-93.
40. Alban Dachauer, S.J., *The Sacred Heart* (Milwaukee: The Bruce Publishing Company, 1959), pp. 147-148.
41. I am indebted to more than one source for historical facts concerning Medjugorje. I would particularly like to acknowledge Mary Joan Wallace's book, *Medjugorje: Its Background and Messages* (Huntington Beach: Follow Me Communications, Inc., 1991).
42. Rev. Richard Foley, S.J., in a talk given at Cincinnati, Ohio, October, 1992.
43. St. Teresa of Avila, *Interior Castle,* translated by E. Allison Peers (New York: Doubleday, 1961), ''Second Mansions,'' p. 51.
44. *Ibid.,* ''Fourth Mansions,'' p. 76.

45. Karl Rahner, S.J., *Do You Believe in God?* (New York: Newman Press, 1969), p. 19.
46. Pope, John Paul II, *The Mother of the Redeemer, op. cit.,* No. 47.
47. *The Documents of Vatican II* (New York: The America Press, 1966), *Dogmatic Constitution on the Church,* No. 7.
48. *Ibid., Constitution on the Liturgy,* No. 48.
49. Pope Paul VI, *Devotion to the Blessed Virgin Mary (Marialis Cultus)* (Washington: United States Catholic Conference, 1974), No. 46.
50. *Our Lady's Peace Plan, op. cit.,* p. 2.
51. *I Am Your Jesus of Mercy,* (Milford: The Riehle Foundation, 1989), Vol. 1, pp. 39-40.
52. *To the Priests, Our Lady's Beloved Sons, op. cit.,* No. 232.
53. *The Gold Book of Prayers* (Milford: The Riehle Foundation, 1988), p. 55.
54. *Ibid.,* p. 46.
55. John Cardinal Newman, *Discourses Addressed to Mixed Congregations* (London: Longmans, Green and Co., 1906), pp. 111-112.

Other Books By Fr. Edward Carter

THE PAIN AND THE JOY
by Fr. Edward Carter, S.J.

By focusing on Christ's example we can live successfully Christian lives and survive against an onslaught of discouragement. Fr. Carter provides inspiring reflections revealing Jesus' answers to life's frustrations.

144 pages **$5.00**

MOTHER AT OUR SIDE
by Fr. Edward Carter, S.J.

An easy to read composite look at Mary's role in our lives. Fr. Carter incorporates this role into all aspects of our spiritual journey through life.

144 pages **$5.00**

Additional copies of this book, or other titles by Fr. Carter may be ordered as follows:

Individuals—contact: The Riehle Foundation, P.O. Box 7, Milford, Ohio 45150. Phone (513) 576-0032.

Bookstores and distributors should contact: Faith Publishing Company, P.O. Box 237, Milford, Ohio 45150. Phone (513) 576-6400, or 800-576-6477.

Please contact the above publishers for a catalog and list of other materials available.

Faith Publishing Company

Faith Publishing Company has been organized as a service for the publishing and distribution of materials that reflect Christian values, and in particular, the teachings of the Catholic Church.

It is dedicated to publication of only those materials that reflect such values.

Faith Publishing Company also publishes books for The Riehle Foundation. The Foundation is a non-profit, tax-exempt producer and distributor of Catholic books and materials, worldwide, and also supplies hospital and prison ministries, churches, and mission organizations.

For more information on the publications of Faith Publishing Company, contact:

Faith Publishing Company
P.O. BOX 237
MILFORD, OHIO 45150